SURVIVING THE DAILY GRIND

SURVIVING THE DAILY GRIND

BARTLEBY'S GUIDE TO WORK

PHILIP COGGAN

Published under exclusive licence from The Economist by
Profile Books Ltd
29 Cloth Fair
London
ECIA 7JQ
www.profilebooks.com

1 3 5 7 9 10 8 6 4 2

Typeset in Garamond by MacGuru Ltd
Printed and bound in Great Britain by
Clays Ltd, Elcograf S.p.A.

A CIP catalogue record for this book is available from the British Library.

ISBN 978 1 78816 924 0
eISBN 978 1 78283 911 8

To all the long-suffering office workers of the world

CONTENTS

PREFACE

I magine that this is the plan for your working day. First, you have a two-hour Zoom meeting in which your manager will outline a "holistic" approach to the company's strategy. Then there will be a call from the marketing team which plans to rename your group the "operational solutions" team. Finally, there will be a mandatory lecture under the guise of your company's "thought leadership" programme. Does the prospect fill you with dread? Do you wish you could create an avatar who could nod sagely and say "quite right" occasionally, to save you the bother of attending any or all of these events?

Then this is the book for you. It is designed for workers who find their job frustrating (but need the money) and for managers who have learned to talk in corporate waffle but wish they could express themselves more clearly. It is based on the things I have learned as the Bartleby columnist on management and work at *The Economist* but also in a 40-year career at organisations, large and small.

The book is not a compilation of columns but, inevitably,

some of the ideas and phrasing will have appeared before in *The Economist*. Writing at book length has given me the opportunity to organise and hone the concepts that sustained the column over the years.

As *Economist* writers are anonymous, the author of the column was always referred to as "Bartleby" and I have maintained this habit in the book. Because the column was about work and management, the issues had touched me directly, so there is much more of the personal voice than is usual for *Economist* writers. This also allows me to take a more offbeat and humorous tone than my colleagues who have to cover such weighty matters as Chinese foreign policy and climate change.

At the end of the book, readers will understand why modern work is organised in a way that can be so frustrating. And the book will also show that things don't need to be this bad; there are ways of managing people that are less bureaucratic, that allow individual workers to be more creative and spend less time in meetings and do not involve language that is seeped through with obfuscation and circumlocution. But enough. This is not the time to "circle back" or "reach out". Let us get on with it.

Philip Coggan
November 2021

INTRODUCTION

It is one of the great mysteries of modern working life. Why do so many managers pollute their utterances with so much inane jargon? When we leave home and head to the office, it is almost as if we have to speak a different language. This language is one of the reasons why work can be so tiresome.

To understand why this climate has developed, we must call on the spirit of the great C. Northcote Parkinson, a 20th-century management writer, who created "Parkinson's law" – that "work expands so as to fill the time available for its completion". This new guide will propose a number of new working laws and amend some old ones.

The first law is: *jargon abhors a vacuum*. All too often, executives know they have nothing significant to say in a speech or to write in a memo. But they are aware they have to say *something* and, furthermore, that they have to speak at some length. So they use long words, obscure jargon and buzzwords to fill the space.

The second reason for managers to use jargon is to establish their credentials. By using these terms in their vocabulary, they feel they are demonstrating their expertise and fitness to rule. Like a priest intoning the liturgy in Latin or a football supporter chanting the team song, their language shows they belong to a tribe.

The manager's colleagues or subordinates are unlikely to challenge them on their use of banal language or impenetrable jargon, for fear of causing offence or revealing their own ignorance. Social convention makes them reluctant to declare that the emperor has no clothes or makes no sense.

Of course, most managers are perfectly decent people. In a sense they are trapped in their roles, just as a heavy-set Hollywood actor will become typecast as a villain. They use the jargon because it is expected of them. For a long time, managers had their own dress code as well; a suit and tie for men, a jacket, blouse, skirt and heels for women. The rise of Silicon Valley casual (T-shirt and chinos) has created more freedom in the last 20 years (although more for men than for women). The language is just another version of the uniform.

Another reason for the flourishing of corporate babble is the ephemeral nature of much modern work. Most modern humans are not hunting game, growing crops or even making physical objects – tasks where the aim is clear and output can be easily measured. Instead most people in the developed world work in the service sector. Some service sector activity has straightforward aims: cutting hair or serving meals, for example. But lots of us work in jobs with titles that would have baffled our ancestors: creative director, logistics coordinator or social media curator. Those who hold these jobs may not be entirely sure how to measure success. So they try to look busy and, in doing so, invent activities to keep their colleagues and subordinates busy.

Thus the irritations of modern working life are not confined to language; they also relate to managerial behaviour. Part of the satisfaction of being a manager comes from telling other people what to do, rather than being told what to do yourself. Power, even in small things, can be exhilarating. If you want subordinates to attend a meeting, you can insist on it; the same goes for evening functions and 7.30am breakfasts. Allowing underlings to miss these occasions would undermine the manager's authority. Chimps grin to gain acceptance and show submission to the leader of the group; office workers show up to their boss's unnecessary meetings to achieve the same effect.

In turn, junior managers are driven by the need to meet the demands of the corporate hierarchy. There is an old rhyme:

Great fleas have little fleas upon their backs to bite 'em,
And little fleas have lesser fleas, and so ad infinitum.

The same system applies in companies, but in reverse. Each layer of management has another layer above it all the way up to the chief executive. And in a big company, the chief executive has to worry about the board of directors and the shareholders. A corporate culture is set from the top. Junior managers may worry that, if they appear too relaxed with their subordinates, they will not be marked for promotion. Business magazines are full of pieces lionising chief executives who get up at 4am to deal with their e-mails; they spare less thought for the poor schmucks who wake to find five messages from their boss before they have had their breakfast.

When managers are uncertain about the usefulness of their own activities, they are naturally tempted to create artificial goals for their teams to meet; boxes to tick and lists to check. It is a long-established rule that too much bureaucracy is a characteristic of bad organisations. The *Simple Sabotage Field Manual*, compiled by the OSS (the precursor to the CIA) during the second world war, had a number of suggestions for managers who want to undermine the work of their team.[1] These include "insist on perfect work in relatively unimportant products; send back for refinishing those that have the least flaw" and "multiply the procedures and clearances involved in issuing instructions, pay checks, and so on. See that three people have to approve everything where one would do."

Other suggestions for sabotage include "talk as frequently as possible and at great length" and "bring up irrelevant issues as frequently as possible". And the OSS manual suggested that the best way to lower morale is to be "pleasant to inefficient workers" and "give them undeserved promotions". If you think that your company is following the manual, you are probably not alone.

So many of the things we find most frustrating at work – the endless meetings, the meaningless jargon – are social constructs, rather than actions necessary to fulfil the required tasks. Indeed, one of the reasons we find these things so annoying is that we know very well that these elements are not useful, and yet they are forced upon us. As Rousseau might have said, had he been born in the modern era: "Man was born free, but is everywhere stuck in a meeting."

C. Northcote Parkinson spotted many of these problems in the middle of the 20th century. He described how bureaucracy tended to propagate itself. An overworked manager will ask to hire two subordinates (not one, because a single underling might become a rival). These subordinates will generate paperwork which the senior manager will have to review, making the boss even busier and potentially encouraged to demand even more staff. This is just one illustration of his law that "work expands to fill the time available".

Work's other compensations

Working life is not all bad, of course, and its appeal is not just the ability to earn money. There is the camaraderie of colleagues. The occasional satisfaction of a task well done. The intellectual stimulation that comes from dealing with new ideas or new people. And, most importantly, work gives our lives purpose: a reason to get up in the morning that does not involve playing video games or watching Netflix.

For these reasons, being out of work is a dismal experience. A study of the long-term unemployed in Germany found that 15.6% suffered from minor depression and 34.4% had major depression. Fatigue and difficulty in concentration were two of the common systems of those affected. Human brains evolved to be active and we get bored with nothing to do. Just as importantly, we get our social status from our job: "What do you do?" is a common conversational opener. Being a doctor normally gets lots of kudos; depending on the social setting, announcing yourself as a banker or gun salesman might not be as popular.

The result is that, even though sometimes we can't live

with work, we keep going because we can't live without it. It is hardly surprising that we find some elements of employment to be tedious and pointless; the same restlessness that makes us bored without work means that we chafe at the constraints of spending a large proportion of our working hours serving the interests of our employers, rather than ourselves.

This book is intended to help ordinary workers survive the daily grind, by allowing them to spot the absurdities and the bullshit pumped out by management, and to find ways to do a good job without losing their sanity. But it is also designed to help managers become better at doing their jobs, by pointing out some of the obvious traps that supervisors fall into. If managers get better, the working lives of ordinary employees can improve too. People often don't leave bad jobs, they leave bad managers.

This dual approach harks back to the Herman Melville short story *Bartleby, the Scrivener: A Story of Wall Street*, which inspired me to name a column in *The Economist* on management and work. The 19th-century story tells of a man called Bartleby who takes a job in an office as a scrivener (clerk) and initially seems very keen. Suddenly, however, he refuses all requests from his boss, saying: "I would prefer not to." No attempts at blandishment, reasoning or threats from the manager could make him change his mind. Eventually the recalcitrant starts living in the office and the firm has to move premises to avoid him; Bartleby ends up wasting away in prison, too lethargic even to eat. In its own way, the story can be seen as the tale of a worker refusing to conform to society's demands by performing meaningless tasks. Alternatively, the tale can be seen as an illustration of the failure of managers to find ways of motivating their staff.

This book will give many instances of occasions where employees would understandably be tempted to say: "I prefer not to." But first, we need to consider how work practices evolved into the current system.

A potted history of work

Work has changed dramatically over the millennia. Anthropologists point wistfully to the days when hunter-gatherers could garner all the necessary food, water and firewood in 15 hours a week, leaving the rest of the time free for leisure. We have only limited information about what they did with that free time – cave painting and jewellery making excepted. They had none of the modern pastimes, from books through TV to recorded music, to keep them entertained. There is vigorous debate about whether life in those ancient times was more violent or less violent, or indeed more pleasant, than it is today. But a hunter-gatherer lifestyle could not sustain anything like the size of human population that exists in the 21st century.

Anthropologists now believe it is humanity's ability to co-operate that allowed us to outpace other hominids. Stronger social networks allowed us to develop better technology which in turn allowed us to feed more people and develop even denser networks. Agriculture enabled the human population to expand substantially but at a significant initial cost. Focusing on a small number of crops made humans less healthy, and at risk of famine. Gathering in large numbers in close proximity to domesticated animals left humans prone to infectious disease. Farmers had to work harder than hunter-gatherers – sowing, weeding, harvesting the crops and converting the grains into bread and other meals. Early agricultural societies were less egalitarian, as grain had to be stored, and thus those who controlled the stores were in charge of the food supply. Over time, land ownership became concentrated among a narrow elite; had you been born a thousand years ago, the chances are high that you would have been a peasant with a low life expectancy.

The emergence of small towns and cities led to a host of new occupations. Some were specialised – shoemakers, blacksmiths and brewers who could take advantage of a large group of customers gathered in the same place. Other people became servants to look after the elite; some were slaves who were regarded as the property of their masters, to be bought and sold without any consideration of their interests.

Until 1800 or so, most people worked on their own, or in small groups. Organised employment was rare. There was no need for management theory or bureaucracy. The textiles industry, for example, operated on a "putting-out" system whereby merchants brought yarn to be spun, or cloth to be woven, sewn or shaped by a largely female workforce, operating in their own homes. People were paid for the amount they produced.

But the industrial revolution changed all that. Machinery was used to spin and weave cloth, and this machinery used water and steam power. The workers had to gather in a central place, the factory, and operate machines owned by the mill owner. They were required to turn up for a shift, often of 12–14 hours a day. Their time was no longer their own. At work, there were strict rules on behaviour, including bans on talking, enforced by foremen or overseers. Many factories recruited women and young children because they were more docile than adult men. Like the emergence of farming, this economic shift also came at a high initial cost. People crowded together in cities with no plumbing or sewers and life expectancy declined sharply in places like Liverpool or Manchester.

Lifestyles also changed as a result. Many people did not own a watch or a clock. So that required a new infrastructure, including "knocker-uppers" – people who went from door to door to wake sleepy workers, and the factory whistle or horn to signify the beginning and end of the shift. In time, this would lead to punch cards to prove that employees had arrived and left on time.

The emergence of trains, and later buses and cars, allowed some workers to commute longer distances to their place of employment, leading to the "rush hour", a concept unimaginable in the 18th century. And the industrial revolution also saw the emergence of large companies, particularly in the rail and energy sectors. These companies needed people to record details such as sales, wages and the supply of raw materials. In turn, this led to "white collar" workers who were grouped together in offices, under the ever-seeing eye of their supervisors.

By the early 20th century, the modern pattern of work had appeared, with many employees working for large companies or the government, working a set pattern of hours (eventually 9 to 5, five days a week) from the time they left school or university to the time they retired. (The word "weekend" was first used in 1879.) And those workers had to deal with a hierarchy of managers, stretching all the way up from the team leader to the chief executive. Big companies tend to have departments that handle different functions (marketing, finance, personnel and so on) and cover different regions and countries. Each required a management structure.

Not every job fitted into this pattern, of course. Some people were self-employed, usually those with a marketable skill such as plumbing. This gave workers more freedom at the expense of less security. In recent years, we have seen the emergence of the "gig economy" in which people are not treated as full-time employees and often lack security or the right to sick pay or holiday pay. At the moment, though, most people are still "wage slaves", as they have become known. And they have to put up with the tedium, the jargon and the idiocies that this book will describe.

The pandemic and after
It is often said that crises do not create new trends in society; they simply accelerate those that are already in place. The covid-19 pandemic looks like being another example of the theory. It will advance the pre-existing trend for people to shop online, rather than in physical stores, and for consumers to use plastic cards, rather than cash, for purchases. And it will also accelerate the trend for people to work remotely, rather than in the office.

Why did so many people gather in offices in the first place? The rationale was that office communication was largely conducted on paper – memos, purchase orders and the like – and people needed to be close together so the paper could be passed around. Managers wanted to keep a close eye on their staff to ensure that they were not slacking; meetings were held face to face.

Given the technology of the day, this was an understandable way of organising things. But technology slowly changed. Some big companies had offices all over the world and they had to communicate via telegram, telephone and letters. By the 1970s and 1980s, the facsimile machine offered a way to transmit documents. But until the last two decades of the 20th century, these forms of communication were either expensive or slow.

The internet, and better broadband connections, changed all that in the 1990s and 2000s. Managers were able to have detailed and instant communications with their staff and their overseas subsidiaries, enabling them to keep track of sales, shipments and stock levels. Documents could be transferred onscreen rather than on paper; there was no need for everyone to gather in the same place.

It took time, however, for patterns of work to change. Most people were still required to endure the rush hour and a long commute in order to turn up at the office at the same time every weekday. In part, this was because working from home was regarded with suspicion; employees were suspected of slacking when not under the boss's watchful eye. Remote workers felt more isolated and were less likely to feel part of the team.

The pandemic changed everything. Suddenly, governments imposed economic lockdowns and offices were closed. Many people were forced to work from home. Managers and employees made the best of it. Employees were saved from the morning and evening commute and worked, on average, 48 minutes a day more than when they went into the office.

The sudden prevalence of working from home shows that changes in long-established patterns of work can occur. So that gives us hope that we can eliminate some of the other annoyances that this book will describe. Some companies do things much better, allowing workers to prioritise the tasks they find most important; some managers are direct and clear when they speak.

Over the course of this book, we will try and help readers cope with the vicissitudes of modern work. We will update Parkinson's law, examine and update the Peter principle (that people are promoted to their level of incompetence) and create new "Bartleby's laws" that will help readers navigate the new world of work. The book will suggest ways of improving job interviews, feedback sessions and corporate celebrations. And it will provide a cynical, but useful, guide to the jargon that managers spout. If we all take the lessons to heart, work does not have to be a four-letter word.

1

GETTING STARTED

Much of this book will discuss the frustrations of working life. But the trickiest problem may be getting a job in the first place.

Interviews

In 2019, a tweet from Olivia Bland, a 22-year-old Briton, went viral. She had suffered what was dubbed the "interview from hell" which left her crying at the bus stop. The interviewer, a man called Craig Dean, scrolled through her Spotify list and criticised her musical choices, made rude remarks about the way she sat and called her an underachiever. Olivia said she "felt like being sat in the room with my abusive ex". The bizarre kicker is that, after all the aggravation, she was offered the job. Wisely, she turned it down.[1]

Mr Dean apologised for any hurt he had caused. But the broader point is that his interviewing technique was severely misguided. Ms Bland's musical preferences were of no importance unless she was applying to be a disc jockey. Interviews should not be a random series of questions about a candidate's personal life since these will only produce subjective responses on the part of the interviewer.

Far too many questions at interviews are pointless. "Where do you see yourself in five years' time?" is a classic example. A few bold souls may be tempted to answer: "Sitting in your place on the other side of the table," but this response is as likely to irritate as impress. Seriously, how can any of us know where we will be five years from now? Another terrible question is: "What do you think is your biggest weakness?" It is tempting not to admit to any faults at all or to come back with a clever-dick answer like: "My greatest weakness is that I'm a perfectionist." But this question is unlikely to lead to an honest answer. Candidates' ability to deal with this query is probably dependent on their ability to lie, or obfuscate. So if they answer it well, the chances are high that they are the sort of person who will mislead their boss when a project gets into difficulty.

Glassdoor, the website that allows workers to rate their employers, published a list of the 50 most-asked interview questions which is worth a glance.[2] Aside from the obvious "Why should we hire you? What are your strengths?" there are tricky questions like: "How do you handle pressure?" and "Where can you improve?" It is considered wise to admit to some shortcomings and then reveal how you are addressing them. Some firms ask if you know the name of the chief executive or their main customers, so best to do some research before you turn up. But it is slightly depressing to see that some ask about your favourite website, or the last book you read, which sounds more like a bad first date than an interview.

Experts generally agree that the approach most likely to result in hiring the best employees, and a more diverse workforce, involves a structured interview. The same set of questions should be asked of all candidates so they can be easily compared. And some of those questions should relate to job attributes like experience or skills. A meta-study of personnel selection methods found that structured interviews were significantly more useful than unstructured interviews in finding productive employees.[3]

An even more rigorous approach is to get the candidate into the office for a while and ask them to perform one of the tasks they are likely to undertake if they get the job. A survey by LinkedIn, a social network for employees, found that one of the most useful techniques was to assess the candidates' soft skills, such as teamwork and flexibility.[4] Many companies use a 20-minute psychological test. A 2017 survey found that 32% of human resources teams used such tests when hiring executives and 17% of them used these tests when recruiting hourly workers.[5] But the tests vary widely in quality and are subject to bias; in 2018, two US companies agreed to stop using their tests after the Equal Employment Opportunity Commission determined that they adversely affected applicants because of their race or national origin.

An ingenious (although admittedly niche) alternative, practised by Walt Bettinger of financial broker Charles Schwab, is to invite the candidate to breakfast. Beforehand, Mr Bettinger asks the manager to mess up his guest's order and then see how the candidate reacts: are they rude or understanding?[6] Presumably tantrum-throwers fail to get hired.

Some companies interview their candidates remotely

on video and then use the services of software companies that offer algorithms designed to assess the jobseekers. The algorithms analyse facial expressions with the aim of determining characteristics such as dependability and emotional intelligence. But in January 2021, Hirevue, one of the leading companies in the field, said it would no longer use visual analysis in its job assessments and would focus on other factors such as language.[7] Psychologists point out that people express emotions in a wide variety of ways, which cannot always be interpreted reliably from facial expressions. Furthermore, since the interviewees know they are being analysed, the process is likely to be artificial; it is hard to be natural when you know you are being scrutinised so closely.

Of course, getting an interview is often the biggest struggle of all. Many multinational companies now use a computer algorithm to sort through the thousands (sometimes hundreds of thousands) of candidates who apply to work for them. This step is inevitable as the companies would need to have vast teams to analyse the applicants individually. In theory, this can work well. An algorithm can be unbiased if designed correctly. But what matters is the information the programmer puts into it. If the ideal credentials are based on the attributes of the current workforce, and most employees are white, male and privately educated, then the algorithm may well pick more people in that vein.

Many jobseekers may fail to get to the interview stage because of the way that they have prepared their resumé or curriculum vitae (CV). Victoria McLean, a former head-hunter and recruitment manager, set up a company called City CV to help job applicants. She says that 75% of resumés may be rejected immediately, often because they lack the key words that the algorithm is searching for. These words often relate to the type of experience the company requires. So candidates should pay careful attention to the job advert and the language it uses; if it mentions the acronym PM (for project management), for example, a qualified candidate should use PM in their resumé. They should also make sure their LinkedIn page has the same details as their CV as employers may well use their entries to cross-check.

Biased hiring

Employment biases can emerge in many different ways. One study found that adverts on Facebook for jobs as taxi drivers and janitors were more likely to be shown to ethnic minority users whereas postings for pre-school teachers and secretaries were more likely to be shown to women.[8] This may well be because those employers who place their ads choose to optimise their search based on how many views (that is, how much engagement) they get; the algorithm may then target those people who have responded to similar adverts in the past.

The wording of job adverts is also important. Research shows that women are less likely to apply for jobs when the adverts use words such as "aggressive" or "ambitious". One company changed its advert to focus on qualities such as enthusiasm and innovation, and used a photo of a woman rather than a man; it found that the proportion of female applicants rose from 5% to 40%.[9]

Racial bias is a significant problem. A study of US job applications found that white people with a criminal record received as many callbacks from employers as black people who had never committed an offence.[10] There is also evidence that employers discriminate based on something as simple as a candidate's name; certain types of forename are associated with African-Americans or Asians, for example. Some applicants may accordingly feel forced to "whiten" their name by choosing an Anglicised version, or by applying with their middle name if it is associated with those of European descent, like David or Jane. Another approach is to add "white-sounding" hobbies like hiking or skiing. A study found that 25% of African-Americans who whitened their resumés got callbacks for interviews compared with 10% of those who did not.[11]

Many companies now have "diversity and inclusion" policies that aim to counteract biases, and will sometimes have an executive responsible for overseeing the issue. One answer on the recruitment front is to have interview panels that are more diverse, on the grounds that people have an innate tendency to pick people like themselves. If the panel is all white and male, it is hardly surprising if those are the candidates they choose. Making sure that there is at least one woman, and one person from an ethnic minority, on every shortlist is another potential approach.

The danger is that companies try to create a diverse shortlist of candidates but only include a "token" representative female or member of an ethnic minority. One study tested bias by asking students to pick a candidate for the post of athletic director; the candidates had similar qualifications but some had white-sounding, and some black-sounding, names.[12] When two candidates were white and one black, the panel tended to pick a white applicant, but this switched when two of the candidates were black. The same pattern occurred when it came to gender; the panel picked a man when two of the three candidates were male and a woman when two of three were female. Another study found that, if there were just one woman in a four-person shortlist, her odds of being selected were practically zero; this rose to 67% if three of the four candidates were female. (Of course, those odds are less than chance would suggest, but it is still a lot better.)

Bias can result from trivial issues. Black hair tends to be curly and requires treatment to straighten it, which can involve potentially harmful chemicals.[13] Many black women opt to wear their hair naturally, or use alternative styles such as braids or coils. But this causes them to look different from white employees and leads to discrimination. One study found that "black women with natural hairstyles were perceived to be less professional, less competent, and less likely to be recommended for a job interview than black women with straightened hairstyles and white women with either curly or straight hairstyles."[14]

Things are slowly changing on this front. In the US, seven states (at the time of writing) have passed CROWN acts, prohibiting "discrimination based on a person's hair texture or hairstyle if that style or texture is commonly associated with a particular race or national origin". In November 2020, United Parcel Service, the delivery group, changed its dress code to allow facial hair and black hairstyles like afros and braids.[15] However, that raises the question of why the group had a hair code for delivery drivers in the first place:

like most customers, Bartleby simply wants his parcels to arrive on time and doesn't mind whether the driver has a mullet or a moptop.

Another bias is against motherhood. A 2007 survey found that businesses rated mothers as 10% less competent and 15% less committed to their work than non-mothers and their starting salary was 7.4% lower than their childless peers.[16] When it comes to being recommended for management, childless women were 8.2 times more likely to qualify than mothers. Remarkably, the odds were the other way round for men. Fathers were 1.8 times more likely to be recommended for management than childless men.

An anecdote by Betsy Holden, who eventually became co-chief executive of Kraft Foods, illustrates the problem. When she was a vice president at the firm, she became pregnant for the second time. "No one has even done this job with two children," her male boss fretted. "How many children do you have?" she asked. "Two," he replied.[17] This double standard is remarkably common.

The need, and indeed desire, to take maternity leave seems to be another problem. This can interrupt the career progression of many women. Unless they return to the office in a matter of weeks, they may find that the company has moved on without them, offering new projects and promotions to others who have remained in the office. But management is not like school, where if you miss a term's worth of lessons, you will find it impossible to pass the exams. If you were a good manager before you had a baby, you're just as likely to be a good manager afterwards.

Even when they are in the job, women can find that

conventions and even equipment are biased against them. In construction and engineering, tools and safety jackets are designed for male hands and bodies, not those of females. Nor has there been much research on the long-term effects of using things like cleaning products on female bodies whereas the effect of inhaled particles on male miners has been studied extensively.[18]

And then of course there is the issue of sexual harassment. A 2017 survey in the US found that 45% of women had experienced unwanted attention in the workplace[19] and the figure for Britain was 50%.[20] This category includes lewd remarks and questions about an individual's sexual history; worse still, 10% of British women have experienced physical assault at work. This is clearly a problem that has been around for generations and women have been intimidated from reporting it to their (largely male) bosses for fear of ridicule or dismissal. The #MeToo movement has encouraged more women to report the problem but clearly a lot still needs to change; some of those who suffer most are in low-paid jobs like cleaning or waitressing. (Some customers seem to think that, because waitresses depend on tips, they have to put up with offensive behaviour.)

Things have improved for those women who do make it to the top of the executive tree; they have the money to pay for childcare. It has helped that many more women have university degrees than 50 years ago, and society is also marked by assortative mating, with high-achieving couples tending to marry each other. Women now comprise more than a fifth of senior executive positions in US firms, compared with 10% in 1996. Some companies are exceptionally accommodating, providing rooms where nursing mothers can express milk, sinks to wash the breast pumps and even courier services to deliver the milk to the baby when the mothers are away on a business trip.

Even within the male gender, there is discrimination. Participants in a study were shown pictures of male employees of a business consultancy, with similar clothes and masked faces. When asked to rank them in terms of team leadership, they rated the taller men more positively. Indeed, research has shown that taller and more attractive men earn more than their shorter and plainer colleagues. Other research showed that square-jawed men negotiated higher signing-on bonuses for themselves than longer-faced round-jawed peers.[21] People seem to have a certain image of a strong leader (usually a man) and defer to those who fit the template.

Changing minds

It can take a long time to shift these stereotypes. But it is worth remembering that, a hundred years ago, there were hardly any women doctors or lawyers. Some men probably thought that those professions were beyond female capabilities. But now that women doctors and lawyers are commonplace, we hardly think about it. The same will become true of women in many other professions.

In 1970, only one in 20 of the performers in the top five US orchestras was a woman. No doubt there were some people who said this was down to innate ability; women were just not as musical as men. But from that decade onwards, orchestras started to use blind auditions in which the candidates performed behind a screen. This approach made it

50% more likely that women would make it through to final selection. To eliminate another potential source of bias, performers were asked to remove their shoes in case the sound of high heels unconsciously affected the selection process.[22]

Many companies have adopted diversity and inclusion policies to try to improve their ethnic mix in recruitment, and to ensure that workers from ethnic minorities feel valued when they do join the firm. These policies seem to work better for some groups than for others. A survey of US workers by Glassdoor found that African-American employees gave their companies a lower rating than average (3.49 out of 5, versus 3.73) whereas Asian and Hispanic employees gave their firms a higher-than-average rating.

Some companies try to deal with these issues by asking staff to take unconscious bias training, which tries to tackle the hidden prejudices that we are reluctant to acknowledge openly or may not even be aware that we possess. (There are plenty of tests you can take online for this tendency, based on the speed of your response; for example, to see whether you associate black faces with weapons and white faces with harmless objects.) The evidence that these courses really change attitudes is shaky. A Harvard study that examined the effect of training on gender bias found a positive change in attitudes towards women in the workforce but little change in behaviour, except among those who were already favourably disposed.[23]

As a result of these studies, some people argue that all this emphasis on diversity is sheer "political correctness" which distracts staff from hiring the best staff available. It makes no economic sense for companies to be racist or sexist, they say. Companies that fail to hire the best talent will be outcompeted by those that do. Indeed, research by Bank of America found that companies with greater gender diversity on their boards were more profitable, and the same was true for companies with more ethnically diverse workforces.[24]

So why isn't the approach universal? One argument is that the causation is the other way round; only the strongest companies can afford to take a more inclusive approach. Another is that, even if a diverse approach is beneficial, the effect may be slow to appear and may be small in the initial years. Managers have many other issues to worry about.

This is not just about ability. For any company that deals with consumers, it makes sense to have a team of executives who broadly reflect the target market. If the team is entirely white and male, its members may not notice if a product is unlikely to appeal to women or people from ethnic minorities, or indeed that a marketing campaign may turn out to be offensive to other groups.

The first days

The first few days at a company can be alienating and intimidating. At one job, Bartleby turned up at the appointed time and day and was sent upstairs to his new department. "Who are you? Nobody told me you were coming," said the team manager. It was not an encouraging start and relations with that manager (who soon left the company) were never great.

Large companies try to avoid this problem by creating a formal structure for new employees, in a process known in the jargon as "onboarding". This may involve a half-day of talks and videos, training in the software needed to undertake the job, a tour of the office or factory, and so on. The team leader may take the employee to lunch to chat through the process. Many companies go further and put in place a mentor or "buddy" who may not be part of the same team but is sufficiently experienced to offer wise advice about the "culture" of the company. It is always useful to know which managers can take a joke, and which are humourless automatons; how long one can take for lunch and when is an acceptable time to arrive and go home; what things can be put on expenses; and which are the nicest sandwich and coffee shops to visit during working hours.

Some companies go one step further by sending employees a welcome pack before they join; at a consumer goods firm, this may contain some of the group's products. Many firms set workers up with a laptop or mobile phone in advance.

Mentoring is another popular approach. Each new employee is assigned to someone more senior, but who is not their direct manager. This need not be the same person as the culture "buddy" where the relationship is likely to be short term. Mentors are people who workers can turn to if they find they are struggling with a project, or with their boss, or if they are trying to figure out the best route to promotion. The junior worker should be confident that the conversations will remain confidential. A meta-study of mentoring found it was effective in boosting the careers of junior staff although informal links proved better than formal ones.[25]

One problem is that senior men may be reluctant to mentor younger women, for fear that the relationship is seen as inappropriate.[26] A survey in the wake of the #MeToo movement found that nearly half of male managers felt "uncomfortable participating in a common work activity with a woman, such as mentoring, working alone or socialising together".[27] And it's not just the men; women can worry about how a relationship with someone of the other sex may appear to colleagues. The easiest way to deal with this is openness; have mentoring sessions within the office rather than outside them, and make sure that everyone is aware that the discussions are part of a mentoring relationship.

But getting started at a company is one thing. The big irritations of working life may be only just beginning, as the next chapter will explore.

2

MEETINGS

Few sentences in the English language can depress the soul as much as: "We're having a three-hour meeting tomorrow." Hapless workers will brace themselves for long periods of tedium, interrupted by patches of irritation and downright embarrassment.

Bartleby's law states that *80% of the time of 80% of people in meetings is wasted.* Many participants will never speak, gazing wistfully at their watches or surreptitiously at their smartphones. Sometimes the topic will be irrelevant to their duties; sometimes the issue may be significant but the discussion is hogged by a few speakers; sometimes employees dare not speak for fear of upsetting their boss by saying the wrong thing.

It ought to be possible to reduce the time wasted by employees by making the meetings shorter. In his book *The Ministry of Common Sense*, Martin Lindstrom, a management writer, suggests that meetings should last no more than half an hour, and he even brings a large clock to his gatherings to reinforce the point.[1] Another rule that he suggests is to bring along a receptacle where everyone must place their mobile phones or other electronic devices. There is nothing more pointless than someone speaking at a meeting while no one else is paying attention because there is something more interesting on Twitter.

Sometimes meetings can last a long time for the best of intentions. The boss could have called the gathering to inform the team of an important decision, such as lay-offs or an acquisition. Cutting such a meeting short will only make staff more uncertain. In these circumstances, the manager should allow time for the team to ask questions and should ensure that they answer all those queries patiently and honestly.

Even when managers have the best of intentions, meetings can still go wrong. Another of the rules of C. Northcote Parkinson was the "law of triviality": "The time spent on any item of the agenda will be in inverse proportion to the sum [of money] involved." There will be endless debate on issues such as the colour of paint in reception, or the precise amount that employees can claim for lunch on expenses. These issues are discussed at length because they are subjects on which everyone has an opinion. When it comes to really meaty matters, such as the strategic direction of the company, many employees will feel they lack the expertise or nerve to stick their necks out. It is up to the person who chairs the meetings to avoid the triviality problem.

A broader problem is that meetings are not just tedious. They can also cause delays to projects because people wait to take action until their decision is approved by the gathering. If a meeting has no clear purpose, it is just a distraction that stops people from getting on with their work.

So why do people attend so many meetings? In many cases, they are simply told to do so, or it is a set part of their daily routine. But even when attendance is voluntary, people may turn up because of FOMO (fear of missing out). Employees worry that, if they are not present at a meeting, decisions will be made that adversely affect their careers. In addition, they may think that a failure to attend the meeting will be perceived as demonstrating their lack of commitment. There are ways to get round this. Bartleby has been known to turn up for a meeting at the start, linger long enough to catch the editor's eye, and then sneak out surreptitiously long before the end. This tactic only works if the meeting is large enough; it is tough to escape unnoticed from a six-person gathering.

A taxonomy of time-wasters

Of course, if you are looking for new ideas, or a proper examination of a proposal, you have to hold the occasional meeting and let the discussion roam freely. But the law of triviality applies; managers should only allow such a free-ranging discussion where the issue is important and where there is a genuine chance of the proposal being amended.

Letting everyone speak brings its own perils. Some people are incapable of letting a meeting pass without a verbal contribution (everyone has a few colleagues like this). They may feel that they need to interject to justify their presence, or even their existence. Broadly speaking, these time-wasters can be divided into various sub-groups.

Anecdotal Alecs. Some people have a story to tell that is related only tangentially to the topic of discussion. Usually, this tale is convoluted and involves a bewildering variety of different names and places that make it hard for the listeners to keep up. Sometimes there is a punchline but often the story peters out, with the rest of the group smiling politely or making amused snorts. Sadly, this polite appreciation only encourages Anecdotal Alecs to tell a similar story at the next meeting.

Buzzword Bills. Some attendees never have anything substantial to say but have learned a few terms and insist on shoehorning them into every discussion. "They're calling it the new paradigm," they might say, before nodding meaningfully and leaning back in their chair. Or they may talk about focusing on the company's "core competency" and "blitzscaling" the growth. These terms will have little relevance to what has gone before, nor will they allow the discussion to advance by even an inch. Instead, these terms will simply rot the souls of everyone else in the meeting, as they feel their lives tick away listening to this nonsense.

Cliché Charlies. These people are close relatives to Buzzword Bills and they do not bother to dress up their inane utterances in corporate claptrap. But they are just as depressing when they talk about "thinking outside the box", "holistic" approaches to problems and "moving the goalposts". Outside meetings, Cliché Charlies pepper their emails with phrases like "reaching out", "circling back" and "going forward".

Impossible Ians. Some contributors specialise in outlandish suggestions that usually involve other people performing difficult or pointless tasks. In journalism, this might involve someone saying: "Let's get an interview with Tom Cruise" or "Let's send someone to track down the Al Qaeda leadership." In other fields, the person might suggest: "Let's get Beyoncé to endorse our product" or "Why don't we organise a global conference to bring together thought leaders to discuss our concept?" Impossible Ians never volunteer to do these tasks themselves.

Pedantic Petes. Bartleby is a bit of a pedant himself but a lifetime in journalism has taught him to confine his smarty-pants tendencies to shouting at the radio or the TV. You will never understand the full horrors of pedantry until you have sat through 15 minutes of discussion of whether the word e-mail should have a hyphen, whether data is plural or singular and how to use a semi-colon correctly. No one except Pedantic Petes care, but in a meeting of more than ten people, you can easily find two of them to debate one of these issues, while the other attendees long for the sweet release of death. Having said that, I don't care what *The Economist* style guide says: stock market is two words. (There goes my pension.)

Tangential Toms. These folk will live up to the law of triviality by seizing on a tiny point in the discussion, like the font size of the memos or the colour scheme of the brochure and drone on at length. As a result, attendees who had thought of making a substantial point in the meeting will give up, for fear of making the meeting even longer.

These co-workers tend to share a couple of characteristics; they love the sound of their own voice and they are selfish enough to waste the time of others. By prolonging the meeting, they are taking all the other participants hostage. They are effectively insisting that their right to assert their opinion is more important than other people's time. If the meeting has 20 attendees, and one person drones on for ten minutes, that equates to more than three hours of other people's time that has been lost.

In a way, these characters have switched round the old adage (attributed to both Mark Twain and Abraham Lincoln): "Better to keep your mouth shut and be thought a fool than to speak and remove all doubt." They feel that it is better to open their mouths and show enthusiasm than to keep silent and risk the impression of apathy. Those who speak too much should also remember the advice contained within "The Rule of St Benedict", designed for life in a monastery: a monk should "restrain his tongue and keep silence" for "death and life are in the power of the tongue".[2] In other words, if you speak for long enough, you are bound to offend.

It is worth recalling the OSS's *Simple Sabotage Field Manual*.[3] Among the steps it advises to thwart an enemy's operations is to "make speeches. Talk as frequently as possible and at great length. Illustrate your points by long anecdotes and accounts of personal experiences." In addition, it advises saboteurs to "bring up irrelevant issues as frequently as possible", "haggle over precise wordings of communications, minutes, resolutions" and "refer back to matters decided upon at the last meeting and attempt to re-open the question of the advisability of that decision". Perhaps some of your colleagues are secretly working for the opposition?

Those of us who like to escape from meetings can be classified as JOMOs, people who have the joy of missing out. If you get a momentary thrill when you hear that an upcoming meeting has been cancelled, you're a JOMO. JOMOs also shudder at the idea of "networking" which usually means making desultory conversation with total strangers in the hope of career advancement: if forced to attend a networking event, they spend their time alternating between wondering if they are boring other people and being bored by them.

Trial by video

The pandemic meant that face-to-face meetings became impossible. And this led to the widespread adoption of the virtual, video meeting. Devotees of sci-fi movies will recall that video meetings were all the rage in the imagined future. But these usually involved communication between a small group of individuals; an astronaut communicating with his family back on earth, for example. Picture quality tended to be excellent and there was no problem with time delays or lost connections. Nor did the Klingons have to raise their hands to be heard by Captain Kirk.

Group telephone calls were reasonably common in business before the pandemic. Many companies would organise a call at which analysts and key investors could question them about their results. Anyone who has ever spoken at an event will also be familiar with the pre-conference briefing; a phone conversation between the participants. In Bartleby's experience, these were often awkward affairs, with the conversation alternating between complete silence and everyone interrupting each other. Sometimes the preparation call could last longer than the time slot of the conference discussion itself.

But the video call is another kind of torture entirely. Of course, the calls have many potential advantages. Managers can keep in contact with their colleagues, or their clients, in other parts of the world without the expense or the hassle of travelling to see them. Given the problem of climate change, video calls should make a modest contribution to reducing carbon emissions. During the pandemic, video calls were a very important way for people to keep in touch with relatives who might otherwise have been completely isolated.

But the reason that companies have so many video calls is that they represent a way to demonstrate that people are busy. This can be particularly important for managers, who can sometimes struggle to justify their existence. At the office, they can wander round and check in with their team, and they can achieve the same effect by phoning. But a direct phone call only demonstrates to a single person, for a short time, that a manager is working. Organise a video meeting and everyone can see how much effort you are putting in. Hence, Bartleby can propose an amendment to Parkinson's law: "In a pandemic, Zoom expands to fill the time available."

Whether these calls are essential for business meetings is another matter. Some believe that a video meeting allows participants to pick up the subtle cues (facial expressions, body language) that are missing in a traditional telephone call. However, Bartleby interviewed Richard Mullender, who had been a hostage negotiator for the Metropolitan Police. He felt that too much emphasis was placed on body language. It is much easier to understand someone if you can hear them but not see them, than if you can see but not hear them. Mr Mullender always preferred to negotiate by telephone.

Video calls also have something unnatural about them. In large part, this is because they require people to stare at a fixed point (the camera on the laptop or iPad). The effect resembles the "hostage videos" that unhappy victims have been required to take part in by terrorist groups.

People complain of Zoom fatigue (other videoconferencing apps are available) after a day of meetings. A study by Professor Jeremy Bailenson of Stanford University found the problem had a number of causes.[4] The first is that meetings involve direct eye contact for long periods, and this is unsettling. In many cases, the speaker's face looms very large on our screens in a way that normally only happens with a romantic partner or someone who is threatening us by invading our personal space. (It is possible to reduce the size of the picture window to avoid this problem.) Another cause of fatigue is that people speak 15% louder on video calls than they do in person (one wonders if this stems from the subconscious feeling that we are speaking to people who are far away). And video meetings tend to stretch out; a survey of Microsoft Teams meetings in 2021 found that the average call was 45 minutes, up from 35 minutes a year earlier.[5]

The second problem is that participants have the strange feeling of observing themselves, and not in a flattering light. It seems that the laptop camera adds ten pounds to your weight and ten years to your age. Many people find it difficult not to keep looking at their image on screen and stressing about whether their face appears fat, their hair messy or their clothes unfashionable. (Bartleby keeps the camera switched off to avoid this problem but Mr Bailenson suggests using the "hide self-view" button which is available on some apps.)

Some feel insecure about the state of their houses, and elaborately arrange their bookshelves to make them look as learned as possible. Not everyone has bookshelves, of course, and that means that family photos, posters or tacky wallpaper may be visible. There is always the risk that a child, partner or pet wanders in at the wrong moment. The potential for such disruption only adds to the stress.

The risk of embarrassment is not just visual. People may try to speak without pressing the unmute button or may make an insulting comment when they think they have been muted. Bartleby once went for a walk during an Economist meeting (which was held on a bank holiday) and discovered to his horror that the sound of his stomping (and heavy breathing) was being transmitted to the whole group. By the end of the walk, he found e-mails, Whatspp messages and even tweets asking him to mute his phone.

A third issue is that a video call usually makes us immobile; we are seated at a desk or a table so the camera can see us. Of course, this happens in real meetings too but there is something rather unnatural about being forced to sit still at home, where normally we might wander about to make a coffee or wash the dishes.

And finally, the fatigue may stem from the feeling of being constantly observed: Big Brother is watching you. If you laugh, roll your eyes or snort at the wrong moment, you risk insulting the speaker or the other participants. With video calls, Mr Bailenson argues that humans have taken a highly natural event – an in-person conversation – and turned it into an occasion that involves a lot of concentration.

Despite the risk of being observed, many attendees look for distractions. One survey found that 85% of British workers were surreptitiously going through their e-mails while on a Zoom call, and 77% were texting on their mobile phones. If you get caught doing that, you will still be less embarrassed than Jeffrey Toobin, a *New Yorker* writer, who was seen by his colleagues on a video call pleasuring himself in a more intimate way.

However, don't think you can escape the camera by heading out of shot. Both Facebook's Portal and Amazon's Echo have functions that will follow you around the room.[6] And for those physically present at a meeting, Zoom plans to capture their faces on camera so they can appear in the gallery with their remote colleagues. A company called Bluejeans has developed an application that allows people to highlight key moments in a video call and record them for others to watch later. For Bartleby, this sounds like an even more dreadful version of those evenings when the neighbours invited one around to watch video highlights of their holidays; one can imagine people saying: "Look at this moment when I crush Jenkins from Accounts with a witty remark!"

Another more benign possibility is "advanced image manipulation" which allows it to appear that participants are following the meeting even when they are not. Perhaps in the future, we will be able to substitute our presence on a video call with an avatar who can mutter "mm-hm" and "yes, indeed" at suitable moments.

Such stratagems will be necessary because meetings are

no less tedious for being conducted online. My former Economist colleague, Adrian Wooldridge, wrote of "Zoom bores" who take ten minutes to make a simple point and "don't think any meeting is complete unless they have intervened at least three times". Worse still, these bores tend to come in clusters so a speech by one leads to interventions by the others.[7] It might be described as mutually assured distraction.

How to do it better

Organisations could start by having fewer meetings. Jason Fried and David Heinemeier Hansson who run the software company Basecamp write: "Taking many people's time should be so cumbersome that most people won't even bother to try it unless it's really important. Meetings should be a last resort, especially big ones."[8] The duo warn against the use of calendar apps, which mean that employees can suddenly find their diaries are full with meetings. Their advice is echoed in Mr Lindstrom's book by a story of a company where employees found that other people were filling up their calendars with meetings, without their assent.[9] The workers reacted by filling their calendars with fake meetings to ensure they had some free time. In turn, this created the need for a paper-based system in which they could log their "real" meetings.

James Citrin and Darleen DeRosa of the recruitment firm Spencer Stuart make a sensible suggestion to avoid Zoom fatigue in their book *Leading at a Distance*.[10] Instead of making meetings 30 minutes or 60 minutes long, have them last 20 or 50 minutes; that should ensure participants have a 10-minute screen break before the next meeting.

One way of reducing the number of meetings is to be

certain in advance about the purpose of the gathering. Jon Baker, author of a book on meetings, says: "Discussion alone isn't a strong enough reason to have a meeting, or to expect it to work."[11] Mr Lindstrom says that the excessive use of meetings is the result of "habit and a passive and widespread acceptance that this is just how things are in the business world".[12]

If the aim is to impart information, the same effect could be sent with a message on e-mail, Slack or other system. If the aim is to discuss a new product or policy, attendance should be limited to those who are really involved. The more people who attend, the more time is being wasted.

Some meetings are genuinely essential and people have attempted for years to make them more efficient, or shorter, or both. At Amazon, founder Jeff Bezos says that no meeting should be so large that two pizzas could not feed the entire group. He also insists that each meeting begins with the participants silently reading a six-page memo that is designed to create the context for the subsequent discussion.[13] The aim is to ensure that all the participants are fully informed about the issue which should mean that the debate is focused on the relevant questions. The beauty of the Bezos approach is that people can usually write more clearly and concisely than they can speak. That should make it easier for the other participants to understand the presentation and it means that everyone is equally informed.

A similar idea comes from Jon Baker whose ideas for improving meetings include sending out an agenda (and reading material) well in advance. His view is confirmed by Maurice Schweitzer, professor of management at the Wharton

School at the University of Pennsylvania, who points out that informing people of the agenda in advance stops people from being caught off guard. When people are taken by surprise, they often have a negative reaction to what is being proposed.

Another common concept is to hold a stand-up meeting in the hope that this will make things shorter. People get uncomfortable if they stand for too long, whereas they can sit for hours with ease. The stand-up meeting is a regular event at companies which use a system called "agile management" where staff from different parts of the firm are organised into teams with the aim of completing a specific task. The daily stand-up will last only 10 or 15 minutes and is designed to make all team members aware of the project's progress.

Some people describe this stand-up meeting as the daily scrum.[14] This term comes from rugby union, although it is an odd choice of terminology. Any regular rugby fan will know that a scrum involves two sets of hefty, sweaty men pushing against each other in a test of strength that often ends with a collapse or a penalty. Very little progress is made in any direction.

Regular users report that such daily stand-ups can still go on for too long and may involve at least one team member logging in at an inconvenient time or finding themselves stuck in an irrelevant discussion.[15] But there is something to be said, in an era where remote working is likely to be more common, to have at least one moment of the day in which the team is all connected, if only for a few minutes. Without it, it is easy for team members to lose motivation and their sense of direction. But a good team leader will ensure that such meetings are kept to schedule.

Longer meetings are occasionally inevitable. This can be torture for some participants. Jon Baker argues that introverts are the people who are most put off by meetings. Some are bored to death by endless PowerPoint presentations ("Now we turn to slide 34") and Jeff Bezos banned PowerPoint presentations from Amazon meetings.

While banning slides may make sense for a small meeting, there is nothing wrong in using visual aids during a presentation to large groups of people. It is hard for people to concentrate if they have only the speaker to stare at, and if you give people written notes, they tend to read the notes, not listen to the speaker. It is disconcerting to talk to a crowd if nobody is looking directly at you, and the shuffling of pages is also an unwelcome distraction.

Another common problem with meetings is that they are driven by the HIPPO (highest paid person's opinion). Once the manager has pronounced on an issue, few people will want to contradict them. By doing so, the boss acts as a dead weight on further discussion. It takes a bold employee to contradict the manager's view. Professor Schweitzer emphasises that it is important that employees with a low status should be encouraged to air their views, without interruption. Many workers fear that, if they speak up, it may count against them when it comes to pay or promotion. If the agenda is submitted in advance, these views can also be submitted anonymously, which may allow for critical views to be expressed. The manager's role should be to sum up at the end.

The main aim here is to avoid what is known as "groupthink", when a team excludes all dissenting views. This phenomenon was first described in 1972 by the psychologist Irving Janis, who used the concept to examine some of the foreign policy fiascos of the previous 20 years.[16] An obvious example was the Bay of Pigs affair, when the Kennedy administration landed a group of exiles in Cuba in 1961 in the hope of overthrowing Castro's communist regime. The rebels were easily defeated, thanks to the lack of US military support. Janis interviewed many of the advisers behind the decision and discovered that, although many of them had doubts about the expedition, they never voiced them for fear of seeming faint-hearted or soft on communism. Something similar happened during the Vietnam war as the Johnson administration committed more and more resources to a hopeless cause.

Groupthink is only one of a range of psychological traits that explain why people make irrational decisions. Whether singly or in groups, people tend to believe facts or opinions that support their pre-existing views, a tendency known as confirmation bias. We are also reluctant to admit that we have made mistakes. In the business world, this can lead to companies pouring more money into loss-making operations in the belief they can be turned around – a phenomenon known as "sunk costs syndrome". A related problem is "loss aversion"; people dislike making a loss more intensely than they like the feeling of making a profit.

One technique for avoiding confirmation bias and groupthink is known as a pre-mortem. This involves the team conducting an exercise to imagine why the project might fail. Each team member could be asked to write down a list of problems that could occur, and then the team will be required to consider what remedies might be appropriate. According to management consultants McKinsey, pre-mortems are more successful at reducing teams' overconfidence than other approaches, as they enable the group to consider a wider range of problems.[17]

The danger here is that pre-mortems may turn into just another form of meeting and add to the congestion of everyone's working lives. So all the above suggestions should be subject to the golden rule that, *overall, businesses should have fewer meetings and on average they should be shorter*. But meetings are not the only source of work-placed irritation. Many of the other problems will be discussed in the next chapter.

3

OFFICE LIFE

Even if meetings could be reformed to make them short and useful, many other aspects of working life would still be a cause of exasperation. Whether it is the office design, technology, the training exercises or the forced social occasions, there are many times when employees will be forced to grit their teeth or tempted to mutter under their breath. Let us start with the office layout.

Open-plan offices

At the risk of stating the obvious, the idea of "the office" exists on two levels. There is the building as a whole that workers refer to when they say: "I'm heading into the office". And then there is, for the lucky few, an individual space, partitioned off from other people, that workers refer to as "my office". This is a personal area, rather like a "study", to which the individual can retreat and which (within reason) they can adjust for their own comfort. From the mid-1990s to the mid-2000s, Bartleby had his own office, and loved it.

But individual offices take up space, and in an era when

property costs are high, they are not in fashion. Instead, employees sit in vast, open-plan areas, where possible on a single floor. Most notably, Facebook's headquarters in Menlo Park, California spreads over four hectares and is designed to seat 2,800 people on a single level.[1]

Cost saving is not the only rationale for this design. Mark Zuckerberg, Facebook's founder, said: "The idea is to make the perfect engineering space: one giant room that fits thousands of people, all close enough to collaborate together."[2] People will be able to exchange ideas with their neighbours and will have the kind of serendipitous conversation with someone from another department that speaks off creative collaboration. Or that's the theory.

The problem, however, as many people who work in open-plan offices can tell you, is that things don't work as neatly as Mr Zuckerberg hoped. Open-plan offices can be so large that workers feel like battery hens. Privacy is also important for productivity; in an open-plan office, you can never be certain that you aren't being watched. They can also be so noisy that people retreat behind their headphones to shut out the distractions.

Not every open-plan office is the same. Some have cubicles with high walls (as in the Dilbert cartoons); some have cubicles with low walls; and some have no partitions at all. Some analyses of employee behaviour lump all three categories together. To avoid this mistake, the authors of one study looked at the London offices of a technology company with several thousand staff distributed over four floors.[3] They found that two factors were important to working efficiency: how many other desks and employees individual workers could see and whether other staff were sitting behind them. Smaller open-plan areas were better; the larger the area, the noisier and more distracting it tended to be. This also affected teamwork: "because the office is so open it feels hard to talk to colleagues in the open-plan area without disturbing everyone", one respondent to the study said.

As for the desk position, people feel uneasy if things are going on behind their backs, so it was better if they were against the wall, looking across the room. Both the size of office and positioning of desks affected employees' perception of their own productivity. So the authors suggest that "designing smaller and more intimate areas might be advisable as an immediate workplace design choice".

How about collaboration? Ethan Bernstein and Stephen Turban of the Harvard Business School analysed interactions between colleagues in two multinational companies that switched to an open-plan design.[4] They did this by giving the participants badges that used infrared sensors to detect when people were interacting, microphones to determine when they were speaking or listening to each other, another device to monitor their body movements and posture, and a Bluetooth sensor to capture their location. In both companies they found that, in an open-plan design, face-to-face interactions declined sharply whereas e-mail exchanges rose significantly. In part, this was because the offices were so open that workers knew that any spoken exchange would be overheard by their neighbours, so e-mail was a more discreet form of communication.

Many open-plan offices now have "breakout spaces" where employees can go to meet, or little "pods" where they can work in solitude. These areas tend to be booked up quickly. By definition, the need for these spaces suggests that open-plan offices are not ideal for either collaboration or concentration. After all, in many work complexes, the executives still have their own spacious offices, often with panoramic views, which suggests that they consider privacy to be a useful aid to efficient working.

In the spring of 2021, HSBC, the banking giant, revealed that it was abolishing its executive offices in its London headquarters and converting the space into meeting rooms. The managers would have to find a desk in the open-plan space like everyone else. One wonders, however, whether the ordinary staff will be that thrilled to find a top executive sitting behind them. It will surely inhibit conversation and lead to awkward moments (when you are talking about the boss only to find that he or she is behind you). And executives need privacy for confidential meetings like career reviews; they may spend all their time block-booking the new meeting rooms for such purposes.

But breakout spaces are only part of the new layouts. Tech companies have pioneered the introduction of little luxuries such as table-tennis tables or hammocks for employees who want to use up some surplus energy or have a rest. The London office of Transferwise, a payments company, even has a sauna. The rationale for these perks is to make the office so appealing that there is no incentive to go home early. For the same reason, there may be a nice café or coffee shop on site; dry cleaners will pick up and return clothes to the office, and so on. It is an echo of the film *Field of Dreams*: "If you build it, they will work."

Shared space: the final frontier

Not all office spaces are operated by a single company. Another model is the "shared office" where freelancers or start-up businesses rent rooms or desks in a space owned by others, like a day hotel for workers. The concept is most associated with a company called WeWork, which enjoyed a spectacular rise and fall in the 2010s. The WeWork strategy involved leasing office buildings, splitting them into smaller units and then offering perks like free beer to entice freelancers or others to lease space. Sceptics often pointed out that WeWork had a mismatch; it leased buildings for long periods and then recruited occupants on much shorter leases. The company attracted substantial investment from Softbank, a Japanese venture fund, and there was talk in 2019 of the company being valued at $47bn.

All this was very odd since shared office space was not a new idea; companies like Regus (now part of IWG) had been offering the product for ages without attracting anything like as much hype. But WeWork was trying to create the kind of vibe that is associated with a fast-growing technology company and had ambitious plans to expand. This expansion involved huge losses: $883m in 2017 and $1.9bn in 2018.[5] But the idea was to make WeWork synonymous with the idea of the shared office; its flamboyant founder, Adam Neumann, sold the right to use the word "we" to the company for almost $6m.[6] (This was the kind of nonsense that should have been a warning sign.)

When the company tried to float on the stock market in 2019, it proved a hard sell to sceptical investors. Mr Neumann was ousted and the float was abandoned. When the pandemic hit, the company lost $3.2bn in 2020 and another $2.1bn in the first quarter of 2021, as revenues plunged.[7] (It did manage to float in 2021 with a valuation of around $9bn, still remarkable considering its losses.) And the idea of shared offices seems likely to survive as remote working becomes more popular and as large companies recruit workers in disparate places and seek small regional hubs where they can hold meetings. In the future, people may divide their work among three locations: the home, a regional hub and the head office.

Presenteeism

Just as important as the way the office is laid out is the company's approach to work–life balance. When an employee joins a company, it soon becomes clear whether the boss expects people to work late into the night, or at weekends, or even whether management feels it is bad for workers to take their agreed holidays. At some firms, there is a culture that, if employees want to get a pay rise or a promotion, they need to work all the hours that God sends. The result is that workers feel the pressure to stay at the office even when they don't have that much work to do and tend to feel guilty if they leave before the boss does. It is a phenomenon called presenteeism.

In a factory, it makes sense for everyone to be present for the same amount of time. If they are not, the production line will break down. Similarly, in a business that offers customer service, enough staff need to be around to deal with demand. But continuous presence is not necessary in many offices, as the pandemic has shown.

The problem results from managers getting trapped into

a presenteeism mindset on their own part. The manager may be reluctant to leave the office if some of their team are still there. But this can be a time-wasting game of chicken; everyone is staying because somebody else is, not because it is necessary. Keep this up for long enough and some people will burn out.

Goldman Sachs is renowned as a high-pressure work environment. So there was little sympathy in 2021 when a junior analyst surveyed his peers and found that first-year analysts had worked an average 95 hours a week, only managing five hours of sleep a night.[8] In addition, 77% of them had been the subject of workplace abuse. Unsurprisingly, 75% of the analysts had sought, or considered seeking, counselling and, on average, the cohort suffered sharp declines in mental and physical health. The company responded by increasing salaries but that shouldn't have been the point; subjecting young people to excessive hours and abuse is a sign of bad management, not workshy recruits.

In any company, there may be genuine emergencies or moments when a project just has to get finished and people have to stay late into the night. However, a regular pattern of long hours is unlikely to be good for anyone: studies show that workers are less effective when they are tired.

Why, then, do bosses tend to have such a stern attitude towards break-taking? Some of this must date back to the old days of the factories when bosses believed workers would naturally shirk unless strict discipline was maintained. There was a risk that workers who did not pay attention would disrupt the smooth running of the production line. This process was widely perceived as dehumanising and was satirised by Charlie

Chaplin in his film *Modern Times*. Workers were perceived as imperfect machines and condemned to the monotony of repeating the same task all day.

The modern equivalent of the production line is life in a warehouse, walking up and down the aisles to find the right packages. In her book *On the Clock*, Emily Guendelsberger described her time working at an Amazon warehouse.[9] When she applied for the job, she was warned that she would have to walk 5–15 miles (8–24km) a day, climb many flights of stairs and that she might have to work nights, weekends and public holidays at short notice. She was allowed a 30-minute unpaid break for lunch and two 15-minute paid breaks. Those who failed to keep pace with the demanding rate of item-picking could be disciplined. Ms Guendelsberger reported that the physical effort meant that many workers needed painkillers, which were available in the company's vending machines.

Amazon responded to the book with the statement that "for someone who only worked at Amazon for approximately 11 days, Emily Guendelsberger's statements are not an accurate portrayal of working in our buildings". However, it did admit that lunch breaks were unpaid, describing it as "industry standard". To a British writer, this is incomprehensible. If you work a long, physically demanding shift, you need to eat, so a lunch break should be a paid part of the job; it's not as if you can go home during a 30-minute hiatus.

Despite these conditions, it has to be admitted that Amazon has been a remarkable generator of jobs. During the pandemic, it hired 500,000 employees worldwide to deliver goods to house-bound consumers and in 2018 it introduced a $15 an hour minimum wage in the US, double the federally required rate. Other employers have had to catch up, which means in effect Amazon is setting the standard.[10] (Of course, many small retailers would say that Amazon's job gains have come at their expense.)

An Amazon warehouse is an example of a workplace where output is easily measured; parcels picked per hour. But for lots of other jobs in a services-based economy, speed is not the only factor. By using shears, hairdressers could probably deal with three times as many customers per hour, but many of the customers would leave extremely dissatisfied with their haircut. If an office worker doubled the amount of e-mails they wrote every day, the result would simply be to waste the time of their colleagues. (As noted elsewhere, the same goes for doubling the number of meetings.)

Research also shows that decision-making gets more erratic when employees have failed to take a break. An ingenious study by Tobias Baer and Simone Schnall for *Royal Society Open Science* looked at the credit decisions of bank loan officers over the course of a working day.[11] The employees usually started work between 8am and 10am, took lunch between 1pm and 3pm, and tended to leave at 6pm. On average, each analysed 46 applications for restructuring loans a day, with an approval rate of 40%. The approval rate declined significantly between 11am and 2pm, before picking up again and dropping off in the last two hours of work. This cost the bank money, since loans that were restructured were more likely to be repaid than those that were not.

The academics who wrote the paper explained that decision fatigue "typically involves a tendency to revert to the 'default' option, namely whatever choice involves relatively little mental effort". As we get tired, we get lazy as well as crotchety. Similar studies have shown that judges are less likely to grant parole before their lunch break (and more likely to do so afterwards) and that doctors become more likely to recommend unnecessary antibiotics towards the end of their shifts. Breaks can thus improve worker efficiency. And this may also be true of creativity. Kevin Cashman of management consultancy Korn Ferry and author of *The Pause Principle*, says that 78% of executives find that their best ideas came in the shower, or while exercising or commuting to work.[12]

Extra time does not necessarily lead to greater output. Remember Parkinson's law, which states that work expands to fill the time available. If we know we are going to be stuck in the office till 7pm, we will spin out the task; after all, if we finish early, we may be given yet another task that will keep us even later. This often means that we literally waste time while at the office, playing solitaire on our computers, reading the newspaper or searching the internet; looking over our shoulders from time to time to check we are unobserved. Then when the clock reaches the appointed hour, we can go home without upsetting the boss.

Working at home has allowed people to avoid some of this subterfuge. We can finish a task at 2pm and then deliver it to our boss at 5pm and sit in the garden (or the park) for the intervening three hours. As long as we keep our phones to hand, so we can check our e-mails and answer any calls, no one need know what we are doing. For this group of slackers, Bartleby proposes an amendment to Parkinson's law. This group has figured out how to deliver a level of output that is acceptable to their bosses without overtaxing themselves. For them, Parkinson's law can be amended as follows: "For the unconcerned, when unobserved, work shrinks to fill the time required."

But as noted, working at home means there is no clear division between employment and leisure time. Some people are always anxious to show they are busy. This group can be named the Stakhanovites, after a heroically productive miner in the Soviet Union. Stakhanovites worry that, if they are not in a meeting or sending an e-mail to their boss, the company will assume that they are one of the slackers and they will not get a promotion or a pay rise. So they keep frantically, and visibly, busy. The Stakhanovites need their own amendment to Parkinson's law: "For anxious home workers, work expands to fill all their waking hours."

Fakecations

Presenteeism affects not just working hours but the annual holiday, or vacation. A five-week allocation is standard in Europe but many Americans get only two weeks when they begin their jobs, adding extra weeks only with seniority. Even then, many seem reluctant to take the time allowed. Instead of an extended break, many Americans confine their trips to long weekends. These must do little to relieve stress as such a high proportion of the vacation time is spent travelling to their holiday destination and back. A longer break is essential to free the mind from all work-related thoughts. Ideally, the worker should avoid all business calls during that period and allow a maximum ten minutes a day to check e-mails (if only to avoid a swollen inbox on their return). They should feel free to read books, swim in the sea, hike up mountains; anything that might recharge the batteries.

The trouble is that many employees are not allowed to relax on holiday. They are dragged into what has been dubbed "fakecations" in which they are asked to take part in conference calls or answer questions about their duties. This is nothing less than a failure of management. If there are questions that need asking, they need to be put to the employee before they leave; after that, their boss (or a colleague) should be responsible for finding the answer. A properly organised company hires sufficient staff to cover for absences.

And managers should not e-mail staff on holiday with a covering note saying: "This is for when you get back." Employees will feel obliged to read the message anyway and that will disturb their relaxation. There is no excuse for this. It is possible to send a delayed message that will appear in their inbox only on their return.

Some US companies, including Netflix and LinkedIn, offer unlimited holiday to their employees. In some ways, it is a welcome approach: treating employees as adults who can be trusted to take the appropriate amount of leave. The drawback is that employees may feel that they will be breaking an unwritten rule if they take too much time off, and many prefer the certainty of knowing the permitted amount of leave. In some cases, employees end up taking less leave after an unlimited policy is introduced.[13]

Overall, the average US worker took 17.4 days off in 2018, more than six days fewer than their annual entitlement.[14] In effect, they were spending six days a year working for nothing. Americans seem to worry that taking a long break will signal a lack of commitment, or that one of their colleagues will seize the chance to move into their territory while they are away. The average American works 400 hours more a year than a German and 300 more than a French person. It is all slightly odd because, back in 1979, Americans and Europeans worked similar numbers of hours per week.

Workaholism

Workaholism in its current form is a modern development. In the 19th and early 20th centuries, many employees were forced to work long hours by their companies (including Saturday mornings). It was more associated with working class jobs than those among the middle classes. Trade unions campaigned hard to reduce the length of the working week, which eventually fell to the 35–40 hours range.

What has changed in the last 40 years or so is that professionals have come under subtle pressure to work longer than their contracted hours while lower-paid workers have been faced with taking extra jobs (or working overtime) to supplement their income. According to the OECD, 11% of workers in the developed world put in more than 50 hours a week (about 15% of men and 6% of women).[15] This extra time is not necessarily good for productivity; in 2013 an analysis found a negative correlation between gross domestic product per hour and the number of hours worked across member countries.

Working extra time is also bad for workers' health. Britain's Health and Safety Executive (HSE) cites six potential causes of stress at work. The first two are when people cannot cope with the demands of their jobs or when they are unable to control the way they do their work.[16] The HSE calculates that work-related stress accounts for 45% of all working days lost to ill health in the UK, with an average break of 24 days per case.[17]

Things are even worse in the US, where 83% of employees say they feel work-related stress. The American Institute of Stress reckons that this leads to 120,000 deaths a year and $190bn of annual healthcare costs.[18]

Just over a third of workers said their main source of stress was their boss. A smart boss will recognise the problem and reassure workers that presenteeism is not required. A smart boss will also realise that a recharged worker will be more productive on his or her return. Breaks can have other uses for companies. After a financial scandal in 2008, Britain's then regulator, the Financial Services Authority, recommended that all traders take a two-week break at some point in the year. That way, the bank could discover any unusual dealing patterns while the trader was away from their desk. (Barings might have detected the fraud committed by Nick Leeson which led to its collapse in 1995 had it followed this approach.)

The best way to avoid burnout is to use some of the tips presented elsewhere in this book (and summarised in the conclusion). If you spend all your time in meetings, make them shorter or have fewer of them. This may not be possible for meetings called by your superiors but it is feasible when dealing with your own team. If your hours are too long and you have any control over them, then reduce them. At the very least, take your allowed breaks.

Work tools

Once upon a time, Bartleby worked in the civil service. This genuinely involved shuffling paperwork. Memos would arrive from another department which required a response, and this in turn would be recorded and filed in paper form. One of Bartleby's duties was to write "Mrs H: please file" on a folder so the office secretary could put the paper in the correct filing cabinet. This may have been tedious but at least the response did not have to be instant.

Electronic communication is much more demanding. Often it is accompanied by a sound effect (a whistle, ping or whoosh) that insists on your attention. Frequently, these messages are banal but by the time you have read them, your concentration has been broken. Studies suggest that it may take nearly 25 minutes to regain your focus after you have been interrupted.[19] And our concentration is broken a lot; a 2018 survey by Adobe found that office employees spent more than three hours a day dealing with work e-mails.[20]

In their entertaining book *It Doesn't Have to be Crazy at Work*, Jason Fried and David Heinemeier Hansson write: "In almost every situation, the expectation of an immediate response is an unreasonable expectation."[21] An academic study found that "the longer daily time spent on email, the lower was perceived productivity and the higher the measured stress".[22]

In a multinational company, colleagues in different time zones cannot reasonably be expected to respond outside their time zones. (Of course, one time zone may be dominant; often workers in the west coast of the US start early in the morning to catch up with those on the east coast, who are three hours ahead.) The growth of remote working is likely to lead to an increase in what has been dubbed "asynchronous communication" but the rest of us might just call "responding with a delay". The benefits of delay is that workers have time, when they start work, to figure out which communications are most important and to think about their replies.

Of course, many readers will think e-mail is old hat; they have moved on to new methods of communication. This creates a new problem: the multiplication of communication channels. It is not enough to send someone an e-mail; now they have to join a specially targeted message group on Slack. It is not enough to send someone a document in pdf form; now it needs to be shared in Dropbox. It is not enough to have to download Zoom for video meetings on your laptop; you need Microsoft teams and Google Meet as well. Do you make your notes in a Word document? You dinosaur! You should be using Evernote instead.

If all this seems confusing, you are not alone. A survey of 3,000 workers in the US and Britain by Cornell University's Ellis Idea Lab, and Qatalog, a technology company, found that 48% made mistakes because they couldn't keep track of what was going on across different tools, and 43% spent too much time switching between different apps. On average, they wasted almost an hour a day trying to find information.[23]

Every workplace has a few people who are keen to sign up for the latest workplace gadget – the kind of enthusiasts who queue outside Apple stores for the latest iPhone on the day it comes out. There is a larger group of employees who would rather stick with the devices and processes they understand. For the latter group, it is irritating that every new application seems to require yet another password to remember, and regular "updates" (also known as marketing efforts) from the company concerned. When a co-worker sends a document in a new format, it is as if they have decided to send you the information in Esperanto instead of English; yes, we can run it through Google translate but we would rather not bother.

The late journalist Patrick Hutber coined an aphorism that "improvement means deterioration", which became known as Hutber's law. Every time that a company upgrades a service to its customers, or changes the way employees operate, things seem to get worse, not better. A classic example was when Coca-Cola replaced its original formula with "New Coke" to compete with the sweeter Pepsi; such was the consumer revolt that it had to relaunch the old version as "Classic Coke".

Companies respond quickly when consumers revolt but humble employees don't have the power to force through systemic change. They just have to live with the consequences when their employer changes the way that they work. Often a change means that some shortcut or workaround in the old system disappears, because the people who designed the new system weren't aware that employees used it. Productivity dips for a few weeks as workers adjust to the new system and find ways to circumvent its most annoying aspects. Usually, this kind of disruption happens only once every couple of years, but many workers learn to dread the upgrade.

Of course, one has to allow for the natural reaction of older workers to be resistant to new technology. But sometimes one wonders if new apps are adopted for their own sake. Take the Slack channel. It makes a certain degree of sense to have all the messages on a particular subject, or for a particular team, gathered in a single list. However, when a worker has to check too many channels, messages can get lost. And a lot of time will be spent switching between the various apps.

Training

Everyone agrees that training is vital if our workforce is going to cope with the challenges of the 21st century. Employees need to commit themselves to a lifetime of learning if they want to be promoted, earn more money or simply keep their existing jobs. So why don't we look forward to training sessions more than we do?

It all depends on the type of training, of course. The modern approach is to conduct more sessions online, particularly for technological skills. This is vital. Because technology and business patterns are changing all the time, training needs to be focused on the skills that workers need to keep one step ahead of the robots and the artificial intelligence programmes. There is a lot to be said for online courses that employees can take at their own pace, and which involve exercises where workers can see what they got wrong. If the company is using a new operating system, or a communications platform, then a "dummy" session in which workers can test the functionality of the system will avoid an awful lot of problems when it goes live.

What is much more problematic is live training. Perhaps it's to do with a feeling of going back to the classroom, an environment most of us gladly escaped when we were 18 years old. We have to sit in rows, pay attention to the instructor and take our breaks only when we are allowed to. There will be PowerPoint slides; there may even be a few snazzy videos. There may be a whiteboard where the presenter will write down our bright ideas (as long as they conform to the agenda). We may have to break up into groups to come up with a plan or a series of ideas. Every banal insight will be turned into a piece of jargon to make it seem more profound. Of course, some good ideas will be unearthed in the course of an entire day. But because those ideas are hidden in a haystack of dross, it will be hard to remember them.

Worst of all are the bonding sessions which usually involve exercises where workers are called up to the front of the class to embarrass themselves. Perhaps they will be asked to name three things about the boss (without mentioning the words "psychopath" or "incompetent", obviously). More likely they will have to pitch an idea and be the subject of withering criticism from their colleagues. There may be a group exercise in which the team is asked to build some kind of device using paper plates and elastic bands, or fall backwards into each other's arms to demonstrate their trust.

If the staff are really unlucky, they will be dragged to an "awayday" event at a hotel. There will be no escape for the introverts among them; breakfast, lunch and dinner will be eaten collectively, and everyone will be expected to turn up for pre-dinner drinks as well. Bartleby remembers one miserable weekend at an Economist event in a draughty hotel when he had a stinking cold; no doubt it was a relief for everyone when he escaped to bed at 8.30pm. That is the only memory that remains of the event, so the training element (whatever it was) failed to stick.

Does any of this work? Younger people may enjoy the chance to have food and drink at the company's expense. But it seems more likely that bonding is something that is created slowly, over conversations by the kettle, shared jokes in meetings and muttered conversations about difficult bosses and customers.

There is something to be said for organising the occasional collective event so that new members can be properly introduced to the rest of the team, for example. And the same goes for significant corporate developments; integrating a new team after an acquisition, for example. But dragging people away from their regular work and home lives needs a proper justification, otherwise it will cause as much resentment as appreciation.

The golden rule for training managers should be: "Is this course really necessary?" In a significant minority of cases, it may well not be.

Enforced jollity

When workers are young, their jobs can be a great opportunity to find friends. That was one reason why the pandemic was harder on younger people; it severely restricted their socialising. Popping down to the pub with your mates after work gives you the chance to gossip about your colleagues and bitch about your boss. It adds to the camaraderie and boosts team spirit.

But these pub trips aren't for everyone. They can easily become laddish, with the conversation dominated by male sports or by rude jokes. That could make women feel uncomfortable or excluded. Any event that focuses on alcohol will not appeal to Muslims or others who don't drink. And if the venue is expensive, that may exclude workers on low wages.

For workers with families, some will still be happy to socialise but many will want to be back home with their spouses, or looking after their children. Sometimes, of course, these after-work events are not optional; dinners to entertain clients, for example. The author Caroline Criado Perez notes that many companies allow workers to put the cost of food and drink on expenses, but not the fee paid to a babysitter; that is a real problem for single parents, who usually have no option but to pay for childcare.[24]

It is best to hold events towards the end of the working day, so that employees with other responsibilities can take part but still get home on time. Alcohol can be available but shouldn't be the sole focus. Food needs to be carefully labelled so that those whose diets are constrained by religion, allergies or views such as vegetarianism or veganism can take part. With all these constraints, it is hard to be spontaneous.

When it comes to online festivities, the idea of Zoom drinks seems particularly depressing. If the group is larger than half a dozen, then it is hard to have a normal conversation without everybody speaking at once. Quizzes can work but they can be intimidating for those who have not memorised the winners of every football World Cup or the flags of African nations. In their book *Leading at a Distance,* James Citrin and Darleen DeRosa of the recruitment firm Spencer Stuart suggest that virtual festive parties would be enlivened by having staff dress up, with a vote on the best outfit.[25] This may work in some companies but a lot of people will find this embarrassing or an imposition. Another suggestion is that colleagues should submit videos of their kids or pets, which seems absolutely dreadful and a recipe for hours of tedium.

Virtual festivities face a particular paradox; it is hard for them to be spontaneous but any organised element can seem contrived. It is difficult to relax if you know that 30 people may be watching your every move and hearing your every word. It makes much more sense to hold a party on those occasions when the vast majority of the staff are likely to be in attendance.

In short, group events are much better organised from the bottom up than from the top down, and they need to be flexible in format to allow for different tastes. On no account should they be compulsory.

If there is a common theme through workplace annoyances, it is that businesses operate under arbitrary sets of rules that result from tradition, or social convention, or because of the whims of top management. If those managers would ask the staff a few questions about what they want, many of those aggravations might be avoided. Listening to your team is a fundamental principle of management.

4

JARGON

"Going forward, the company plans a game-changing approach to leverage our impact in the customer-facing space and maximise our USP." If your business sends out communications like this, you are not alone. Some workers even play a game called "buzzword bingo" (or, less politely, bullshit bingo) when their boss makes a presentation, crossing off the waffly terms on their cards when they are used.

Everybody mocks the use of business jargon but it continues to multiply. Perhaps this is inevitable. If you work for a company, some jargon terms are bound to creep into your vocabulary if only because your boss and colleagues will be using them. As we learned in the introduction, jargon abhors a vacuum; it exists to fill holes in conversations when people have nothing sensible to say.

Of course, language changes all the time and some of our reaction to new terms may simply be conservatism. (Bartleby admits to being a grumpy old man on occasion, as readers may have guessed already.) New technology does throw up new words and some of the jargon terms described below have been coined to describe particular types of business or market. The problem is that many managers scatter these terms in their normal conversation to create the kind of meaningless mess that is dubbed a "word salad".

Jargon is a little like the private languages used by siblings or groups of friends; a collection of in-jokes that are designed to exclude outsiders. Being a manager can be stressful and exhausting, with the boss frustrated by orders from on high and resistance from below. Sometimes, after a day of meetings, managers must wonder what they have achieved. The imprecision of jargon acts as a shield; it is easy to claim progress, or disguise the lack of it, if one uses woolly language. Take for example this sign-off in an e-mail from a public relations company: "We are accelerators of positive impact for people and planet."

In addition, the use of jargon gives status to managers because they are using language others cannot understand, as if they are medical professionals discussing the terms of obscure ailments. This must be an important job, they hope others will believe, because of the fancy terms they use.

A significant element of jargon is the use of more convoluted language to describe a simple concept. The aim is to make any insight sound sophisticated, rather than trivial or banal. Every time one hears or reads such phrases, the mind goes to George Orwell's rules for clear writing which include: "Never use a long word where a short one will do" and "Never use a foreign phrase, a scientific word or a jargon word if you can think of an everyday English equivalent."[1]

At its worst, this obsession with jargon causes those who write about business to tie themselves in metaphorical knots.

A management report from Oliver Wyman in 2019 carried the headline "It's time to drive impact" which, as a phrase, was a masterclass in meaningless waffle.[2] Normally, combining the words "drive" and "impact" in the same sentence would have unpleasant consequences. The subtitle of this report was "How do we reset healthcare's trajectory?" which raised a whole new set of questions about mixed metaphors. The point in an object's trajectory when it has maximum impact is when it crashes.

Worst of all, managers who use jargon reveal a weakness; if they cannot express themselves clearly, the chances are they don't know what they are doing. A fascinating piece of research by Nomura, a Japanese bank, found that companies that used simple language in their earnings reports achieved share price outperformance of nearly six percentage points a year relative to those which used the most complex language.[3]

In theory, it should help workers if they understand what their managers are blathering on about. In that spirit, here follows a quick, but not exhaustive, guide to the most irritating and mystifying elements of modern business jargon.

Actioning. A fancy word for doing. The first of many examples of a noun that has been turned into a verb or, in this case, a participle (an adjective made from a verb).

Agile. This is a term that dates back to the "Agile manifesto" drawn up by a group of software developers in 2001. The idea was that software was best developed by small interdisciplinary teams, rather than by large groups organised in a rigid hierarchy. A small group can be flexible and respond to changing circumstances, such as customer feedback. As far as software goes, that may be fine but now so many managers want to be "agile" that business discussions sound like a gymnastic event.

Architect. A perfectly good word to describe a person who designs buildings. It is not a verb so don't use it as one.

Bandwidth. Another way of saying "area of expertise, competence or capacity". When first coined, it was probably a smart metaphor; bandwidth is a computing term for the maximum rate of data transfer. It is also applied to people who are overworked: "He doesn't have the bandwidth at the moment." But it has become annoying through overuse.

Blitzscale. This means "expand the business quickly". The idea is that, in some sectors, there are huge advantages in being the first brand to be recognised by the public (also known as **first mover advantage**). For example, Uber expanded rapidly in the minicab market, and the firm became synonymous with hiring a car using an app. Mark Zuckerberg, the chief executive of Facebook (now Meta Platforms, a terrible piece of jargon in its own right), had the motto "Move fast and break things." Wise managers forget about achieving short-term profits and focus on rapid expansion. A reasonable concept if you run a Silicon Valley start-up; less so if you are the sales manager of a widget company.

Blue-sky thinking. This is the kind of phrase used by

managers who have no idea what to do next but would like to demonstrate that they have intellectual flexibility (see also **thinking outside the box**). Also used as a verb, as in: "Let's blue-sky this," which is even worse.

Braindump. A term meaning to pass on knowledge or information. For those who know the English slang term "take a dump", it has unpleasant connotations. It certainly implies that the person has made no attempt to select or refine the facts being delivered.

Brand architecture. Dreadful phrase used by a company to describe its different products.

Burning platform. A tasteless metaphor used to describe a situation where the business needs to undergo rapid change. It dates back to an oil rig disaster where some men survived by jumping into the sea. As 167 people died in the incident, it is grossly offensive to compare it with a company deciding whether to abandon an old product and launch a new one.

Buy-in. This means "get acceptance from", as in: "We need buy-in from the sales department for this project." It is simpler just to say "approval".

Cascade. This word is used to describe "passing information down the hierarchy". It is meant to sound like a positive experience but it may mean either that staff have to listen to meaningless mumbo jumbo, or that they hear half-digested rumours from the high-ups. The phrase brings to mind the quip from the film *The Outlaw Josey Wales*: "Don't piss down my back and tell me it's raining."

Change agent. The kind of phrase used by people who want to sound go-getting or dynamic. "I'm a change agent in this company," they will proclaim. Will remind many Britons of those machines in amusement arcades that supply the money you need for the games.

Circling back. In a message, this is code for "I have decided to bother you again, even though you have showed no interest in my previous communications."

Community. An example of the needless practice of adding words to make a term sound more portentous (see also **space**). So people don't refer to the elderly but to "the elderly community", "the youth community" or "the vegan community". Perhaps we should call people who use the term "the community community"?

CSR. This stands for corporate social responsibility. Companies that emphasise CSR try to avoid negative things (polluting the environment, for example) but also pursue positive aims such as allowing workers to volunteer for charities, paying a fair price to suppliers and so on. See also **ESG**.

C-suite. Where the top executives sit. All their titles start with "c" as in chief executive officer, chief operating officer etc. These titles are multiplying so companies now have chief technology officers, chief diversity officers and even mysterious jobs like chief impact officer and chief observance officer.[4]

Cutting edge. Quantum computers, mRNA vaccines – these are the kind of technologies that are genuinely at the cutting edge of development. A new shampoo, or accounting software, does not come anywhere close to meeting the definition.

Deep dive. A phrase used to describe someone making a close examination of a subject. It doesn't make a lot of sense as a metaphor. If you're going underwater, it's hard to see and you need specialist equipment to stay there very long.

Disintermediating. Cutting out the middleman. If a manufacturer decides to sell goods directly to the customer, rather than via a shop, it is "disintermediating" the retailer. As with many words that mix two prefixes, this is an off-putting mouthful.

DNA. This has rapidly become a shorthand for describing a company's culture, as in: "Helping customers is in our DNA." The term is regularly mocked in the satirical magazine *Private Eye*. Apart from its irritating ubiquity, the problem is that companies don't "inherit" genetic changes from parents or indeed have children to pass these mutations on to. So the biological metaphor is just wrong.

Downsizing. A terrible euphemism for firing people. Sometimes managers use "rightsizing" instead, which is even worse.

Dynamic. Thrusting executives often use this adjective to describe themselves (while others might describe them as "loud and annoying"). But it is also used as a noun, as in "the customer dynamic", which is just a pompous way of saying "dealing with customers".

ESG. This acronym stands for environmental, social and governance which are three factors considered by investors who want to back companies with a good ethical record. The "social" bit refers to how they treat their workers, whether they hire women and people from ethnic minorities and so on. Governance covers issues like how the executives are paid, whether the business avoids tax etc. There is nothing wrong with investors focusing on these issues but there is a tendency to rely on "box-ticking" exercises, in which companies make sure they have conformed to a checklist of these criteria. And the term ESG, when thrown into sentences, is bound to confuse outsiders.

First mover advantage. What a company gains by beating its rivals to a new market opportunity. Only works if customers are interested in the opportunity and the market is profitable.

Future proof. Make the plan immune to new developments. As the future is unknowable, it is impossible to do this. That doesn't stop people from saying it.

Game-changer. A development that dramatically alters the prospects for a business or a product. There are far fewer genuine examples of this than managers seem to think.

Perhaps symbolically, the same is true of sport's most famous example; the moment in 1823 when William Webb Ellis picked up the football and ran with it, supposedly inventing rugby in the process. The claim did not emerge until after Ellis's death in 1872 and the code of rules for rugby football was not written down until 1845.

Goal-oriented. In other words, aiming to do stuff. Another term which is added to pad out a sentence. The point of coming to work is to achieve some goals although if your boss keeps rabbiting on about being "goal-oriented", your main goal may be to find another job.

Going forward. Two words that are added to make a sentence longer and rarely add value. Another way of saying "in the future" and, as such, a statement of the bleeding obvious. If the manager is declaring an intention to do something, they obviously mean to do it in the future. Nobody ever uses the phrase "going backward".

Hard stop. A definite end to a meeting, as in: "We have a hard stop at 5." But the term tends to make the mind think of the end of a car chase involving the police.

Holistic. This literally refers to the idea that one must deal with a whole system, rather than focus on the problems of the individual parts. The term seems to have wandered into the world of business from its use in alternative medicine. There is, of course, nothing wrong with the idea that, when dealing with problems in one area, managers have to consider the repercussions elsewhere. And if you think about it, such an approach is obvious; set the sales department a target based on volume and they may end up selling products at a loss. But the term is often used as a "ten-dollar word" to make the speaker sound sophisticated. It rarely adds any value to the sentence.

Human resources. Dreadful term used for people who used to work in something called the personnel department. Makes one want to adapt the mantra of the 1960s TV show *The Prisoner*: "I am not a resource. I am a free man."

Ideation may be an off-putting word but it has been a medical term for the "formation of ideas or images" since the early 19th century.[5] In business, it has come to favour in the 21st century as a portmanteau word for "idea generation". Essentially, it means the same thing as "brainstorming" but sounds more scientific because of the "tion" ending.

Learnings. A horrible example of the tendency to make verbs into nouns (and vice versa). If someone uses the word, ask them: "Do you mean lessons?"

Leverage. The remarkable properties of levers were known to the ancient Greeks. "Give me a place to stand, and a lever long enough, and I shall move the world," said Archimedes. Leverage is also a technical term in finance, relating to the amount of debt an organisation has taken on. But, in management jargon, the concept of "leverage" is now lazily used to mean "exploit", as in: "We can leverage our expertise in the chilled goods market." If Archimedes had to listen to modern managers misusing his concept, he would find a place to stand that was as far away as possible.

Metrics. It's just an alternative word for "measures" or "criteria" such as sales growth and customer retention. Phrases like "we're exceeding all our metrics" are incredibly annoying.

Ninja. It is hard to see how a Japanese warrior, and staple of martial arts films, can have much relevance to modern commerce. But in a trawl of British job adverts in 2019, Bartleby found requests for "a call-centre ninja", "a black-belt prioritisation ninja" and one post demanding "a ninja-like attention to detail". It is tempting to suggest that candidates dress in black and sneak into the hiring manager's home at night to prove their innate ninjaness but that seems a risky strategy.

Onboarding. Term used by those in human resources departments for the process of settling new employees into the firm. This leads one to imagine that offering new employees a drink is waterboarding. It is clearly a reference to getting on or off a ship or a plane but if that is the case, why isn't the term "boarding"? To make things worse, there is now a tendency to describe the last few months of a company as "offboarding". (Incidentally, isn't the word "deplaning" a really annoying way to describe getting off a flight?) Joining and leaving seem simpler substitutes.

On my radar. A useful phrase for an air traffic controller, but not for a work colleague. It just means "I'm aware of it" or "I'm planning to deal with it," with the clear implication "but not right now".

Open the kimono. To reveal sensitive information. Given the cultural connotations, this phrase is definitely one to avoid.

Paradigm shift. A term devised by Thomas Kuhn to describe a change in scientific approach, such as the emergence of relativity and quantum mechanics. In business, it can be used to describe a fundamental economic or industrial change, such as electrification or the internet. Again, the phrase is massively overused: if Bartleby had a pair of dimes for every time he heard the word "paradigm", he'd be a wealthy man.

Purpose. A word used to describe the ultimate aim of a company. It is tempting to think in many cases this should read "make as much profit as possible" but it is usually something a lot grander and involves saving the planet or bettering the lot of mankind.

Reach out. Shorthand for "I've decided to contact you again, whether you like it or not." As someone pointed out on the internet, this phrase can only be used if you are a member of the classic Motown band *The Four Tops*. (See also **Touch base**.)

Solutions. Another word that is added to make an ordinary activity sound more sophisticated (see also **community** and **space**). A shop doesn't sell carpets, it sells "floor covering solutions". A car dealer offers "mobility solutions" and the marketing department calls itself "client solutions" and so on. Perhaps a company that dissolves things in water claims to offer "solutions solutions".

Space. In the 21st century, space has ceased to be the "final frontier" and has become the first resort for jargon lovers who want to sound sophisticated. They simply take any area of life and add the word "space" to it – as in the "retailing space", "marketing space", and so on. The only function of the word is to fill space and demonstrate the vacuity of the user (see also **community**).

Stakeholders. People who are affected by what the business does. This includes the staff, suppliers, customers and the wider public, given that most businesses affect their community in some way (traffic in the streets, air pollution etc). The term came into use to try and combat the assumption that businesses only owe a duty to their shareholders. It can be an annoying term but it is hard to think of a better one to describe the category.

Stay in our swim lane. Stick to what we do best, in other words. Before using the phrase, remember that people who stay in their swim lane go back and forth and get nowhere.

Sustainability. Another term from the stable that gave the world CSR and ESG. A business is deemed to be sustainable if it can "meet the needs of the present without impairing the ability of future generations to meet their needs". This is usually related to environmental issues (recycling, using renewable energy etc). But some argue that acting immorally (exploiting workers, selling harmful products) is not a sustainable model. A lot of businesses blather on about sustainability but few have achieved it.

Synergy. The idea that combining two companies, or divisions within the same company, can result in better profits. Mainly this comes in the form of lower costs (the combined company doesn't need two payroll divisions, for example) so "synergy" is often a weaselly way of describing more redundancies. And it is true that cost savings can be achieved. The problem is that those savings are often outweighed by the confusion caused when two companies are combined – the turmoil as managers compete for jobs within the combined unit and the clash of cultures that can lead to loss of employee morale.

Takeaway. You might think the manager is talking about a chicken balti or pepperoni pizza. But actually they mean the crucial concept or fact they want you to "take away" from a meeting. Only then do you realise you have sat, bored, for an hour, just to learn about one thing, when a 50-word e-mail would have delivered the same information.

Take it to the next level. This could simply mean: "Let's move this project on to the next phase." All too often, it just means: "Let's have another long and tedious meeting on the same subject."

Take this offline. In other words, can we talk on another occasion? This may be a phrase to use when you are communicating electronically, but it is an odd thing to say in a face-to-face meeting.

Thinking outside the box. Arguably, one of the top ten most annoying phrases. Where is this box? Who thinks in boxes anyway? The term seems to derive from a logic problem called the "nine dots puzzle" which required solvers to connect all the dots with straight lines, without ever lifting the pencil from the paper. The solution requires the participant to start the lines outside the "box" formed by the dots.[6] Although a neat puzzle, it is hard to see how this helps a salesperson to flog toasters in Tasmania. Nor indeed does it help a manager to distinguish an innovative proposition from a wacky, implausible plan.

Thought leadership. A mindlessly annoying and self-aggrandising phrase that often refers to the conference division. Would Aristotle have described himself as a thought leader? Unless you are Bertrand Russell or Albert Einstein, avoid the term.

Touch base. Another phrase that has come adrift from its original moorings; the need for a runner in baseball to touch the base before the player can advance. But it is now used as a synonym for "make contact with". Whereas touching base in baseball is an essential part of the game, in business it often relates to some pointless marketing inquiry.

Valorise. This is a term used in Marxism to describe something that yields its value. It seems to be creeping into corporate jargon as a way of saying "give value to" or as a synonym for "validate".

Value proposition. What the business is offering its customers. As such, it is essential that a company should understand what it is. When dealing with actual customers, however, it is a term best avoided. "We're cheaper" or "We offer better quality and more choice" are much clearer statements.

Vertical. Often used as a term for a niche market (like organic food) since the market may be deep but will be very narrow. In contrast, a company serving a horizontal market is targeting a wide range of potential customers. One of those terms that can be useful since it can clarify what a business is trying to do, but is confusing when used in general conversation.

Wheelhouse. Bartleby received an e-mail that began: 'I know this particular project may not be in your wheelhouse." It clearly refers to an area of expertise, or interest, but the usage was a complete mystery. The captain of a ship may stand in a wheelhouse, but his or her expertise extends far beyond it; the state of the sea, the route that needs sailing etc. It turns out the term was adopted by baseball and refers to the prime hitting area of the batter.[7] But in business, it is just another pointless term.

Readers may have their own disliked terms to add to this list. It is helpful to know what they mean but so many of these jargon terms are like static on the radio; pointless noise that gets in the way of the actual message from the management. But perhaps we should have sympathy; it is time to consider why a manager's life is so difficult.

5

WHO WOULD BE A MANAGER?

Never in the course of human history have so many people been called managers. Read as many histories of ancient Rome and Greece as you like, and you will struggle to find much discussion about the subject of managing the affairs of large numbers of people. There were generals, priests and emperors but few people who might be classed as managers.

But now managers seem to be everywhere. Every week, more tomes are published about the best way to manage people. Of course, it is possible that this will be one of history's temporary phases and managers of large offices will go the way of blacksmiths and alchemists. In the middle of the pandemic, Bartleby had to return to the office of *The Economist* to fetch some books and papers that he needed so he could work at home. Entering the deserted building, it was tempting to imagine what a future archaeologist might say, when asked to speculate about the purpose of such places.

In this era, humans spent the day in glass booths, where they could be observed at all times. At some points in the day, they gathered together for religious services in "meeting rooms" where a priest called a "manager" recited the liturgy and handed out their penitential tasks for the rest of the day. Only when their tasks were complete could they return home to sleep.

The idea of the office as a spiritual site has something to it. Think how medieval monks spent their days. They woke early, gathered for religious services, devoted their time to copying ancient manuscripts or working in the garden to produce food before retiring to bed and starting all over again the next morning. It all sounds a bit like the treadmill of the modern office worker (although religious devotees were spared the commute). There was a recruitment process in which novices trained to become monks, a set form of dress, a code of conduct and even a retirement scheme (elderly devotees were looked after by their fellows). Their daily activities might seem meaningless to us but our daily activities would probably seem meaningless to them.

Managers also act as priests in the sense that they hear our confessions when we have made mistakes, punish us when we stray from the chosen path and offer us benediction in the form of praise, and sacraments in the shape of an annual bonus or a promotion. Outside our families, our relationships with managers are among the most important in our daily lives. Get on badly with the boss, and we are likely to be stressed and unhappy. This gives managers outsized power over us and some are all too aware of it. As the author has already noted: "People don't leave bad jobs; they leave bad managers."

Updating the Peter principle

Becoming a manager is an odd business. Bartleby has spent much of his career in journalism where it is common for reporters to be promoted into management roles. But there is no real relationship between the ability to write well and the ability to manage people. Indeed, it is quite possible that the skills are negatively correlated; writing can be a solitary business, and scoop-getting occasionally requires journalists to "do the dirty" on their sources (reveal information that may reflect badly on them, or their organisations). Neither of these qualities transfers naturally to management. But people have mortgages to pay and children to feed, and naturally they chase management jobs because they pay better.

This chase may be doomed in the long run. In a book published in 1969, Lawrence Peter established the Peter principle: that workers get promoted until they become incompetent.[1] If you are good at your job, you get promoted; if you are bad at your job, you don't. So any manager who has been in his or her post for a significant amount of time is likely to be bad at their job.

A variant of this principle was discovered in a study of almost 40,000 salespeople across 131 firms.[2] The study's authors found that companies have a strong tendency to promote their best salespeople into management roles. But the ability to persuade others to buy goods and services, although extremely useful, is not the same as possessing the strategic planning and administrative competence needed to lead a sales team. Indeed, the study found that past sales performance was in fact a negative indicator of managerial success. The sales records of workers assigned to the previous star performers was 7.5 percentage points lower than for those workers whose managers were weaker at pushing products.

In other words, promoting a star may result in a weaker team as well as a weak manager. To avoid this problem, Scott Adams, the cartoonist, put forward the "Dilbert principle" named after the hero of his comic strip. In his world, the least competent person is promoted to be manager, on the basis that the firm doesn't want to lose somebody on the team who actually does something useful.

Bartleby would like to propose a different variant on the Peter principle, based on the idea that promotion may turn out to be the long, slow path to unhappiness. Promoted people cease to do the part of their jobs that they enjoy: teachers who become headmasters or headmistresses do less teaching, engineers who become heads of department tackle fewer practical problems and so on. The *Bartleby curse* is that people get promoted until they reach a level when they stop enjoying their jobs. At this point, it is not just their competence that is affected; it is their happiness as well.

In part, this is because being a good manager is hard to define. Even in areas where the criteria seem obvious, such as the sales department, the answer is not necessarily clear. A sales manager may be doing well only because the company's product is superior, in which case the kudos may belong to the design or research manager. The company cannot run a counterfactual; rewind the clock and see how sales would have grown with a different manager. Similarly, it might seem a sign of terrible management if a department has high staff turnover but that might be due to conditions elsewhere: rival firms may be on a hiring spree. Another problem is that, in big companies, there are several different layers of management. Is staff morale low (or high) because of the middle managers or because of the top executives? The suspicion is that the top executives get the credit when things go right and the junior managers get the blame when things go wrong.

Similar problems emerge when commentators talk about the qualities required for good leadership. The "halo effect" is a well-known phenomenon. If a business or a manager is successful, they are likely to be ranked highly by others across a whole range of qualities; if they are unsuccessful, their rankings will suffer. A successful leader is decisive; an unsuccessful leader is dictatorial, but these are simply different characterisations of the same personality traits. As Dennis Tourish points out, it is relatively easy to find examples of behaviour that might be associated with good leadership, such as hard work or approachability, and then to cherry pick some examples of top bosses who displayed such qualities: hey presto, one has a theory of leadership (and perhaps a best-selling book). A study of 110 papers in top journals on leadership found that the majority failed to be clear about the criteria needed to define the qualities of a good leader.[3]

It may not be you

Not everyone is suited to becoming a manager. It often seems that a certain type of person is tempted to apply for the role; the person who was a prefect at school or a secretary of a college society. Many workers are tempted to leave the management jobs to such people as they seem so keen. But the keenest individuals may not be the best candidates for the job.

For new managers, disillusion can set in quickly. All too often, an employee swaps a role where the output and impact of their effort are measurable for one where the outcome of their work is ephemeral; at the end of a long day of meetings and phone calls they wonder what they have achieved. The strategic direction of the company is set by those above them; the real work is done by those below them. This may not be very satisfying.

In some cases, teams may be too large for the managers to control. There is a limited number of people with whom we can have close relationships. Robin Dunbar, an anthropologist at the University of Oxford, says that people tend to have five intimate friends, 15 or so good friends, around 50 social friends and about 150 acquaintances. The Special Air Service, Britain's elite fighting unit, has four-man patrols; when your life depends on it, you need to have absolute trust in your colleagues. As a result, such groups are strictly limited in size.

That may explain why most managers are in charge of relatively small teams. And they can be squeezed from both directions, trying to meet the demands of their bosses while keeping the respect of team members. The role can be highly stressful. This was demonstrated by a viral LinkedIn post in the spring of 2021 from Johnny Frostick, who worked as a contractor for the banking institution HSBC, managing a team of 20.[4] Mr Frostick , who was 45, suffered a heart attack on a Sunday as he was preparing for the next day's work; his first thought concerned the meeting with his manager, scheduled for the next day, and the inconvenience his attack would cause the boss. During the pandemic, he had worked 12-hour days during the week, spending most of the time on

Zoom and had to work part-time at weekends as well. The attack made him rethink his priorities, vowing to spend more time with his family and less time on video calls.

Charles Handy, the veteran management theorist, had an early epiphany when working for Royal Dutch Shell, the oil giant. "In exchange for the promise of financial security and guaranteed work, I had sold my time to complete strangers with my permission for them to use that time for their own purposes," he recalled.[5]

More generally, a survey of 1,007 British managers by a medical care provider in 2021 found that 61% had suffered burnout during the pandemic, with 20% feeling that the strain was sufficient to make them consider resigning. Lack of sleep, limited social interaction and working longer hours were among the main factors mentioned.[6] It is easy for a manager to feel trapped in their role, unwilling to slacken their pace because it will set a bad example to their team members and unable to admit the strain to their bosses for fear that they will lose the opportunity for promotion.

This split role causes stress in another way. Often managers will spend more time with their teams than they will with their superiors. And managers, like most people, want to be liked. Occasionally, however, they will have to pass on unwelcome news to their subordinates. Some will be able to harden themselves to the task. But it is unpleasant to tell someone you like that they are not receiving a promotion or a pay rise or, worse still, that they are set to lose their job.

Another problem that all managers face is the kind of petty corporate rules that make their life more difficult. In his book *The Ministry of Common Sense*, Martin Lindstrom recounts the tale of a senior banker who pinned a crayon picture, created by one of his children, on the office wall.[7] The next day, he arrived to find a notice, attached to the picture declaring in capital letters that "YOU ARE IN VIO-LATION OF GROUP POLICY" for not storing items in his desk. The effect of this pointless regulation was to enrage and demotivate the banker concerned.

Often the most frustrating rules concern business travel. Companies have policies that employees (including managers) must use certain airlines or hotel chains or must travel in a particular way. The result can be that managers end up taking longer to get to their destination, or stay miles away from their clients or conference venue. Even if the employee can get a business-class seat that is cheaper than economy class, the rule may forbid taking it. In another of Mr Lindstrom's anecdotes, a junior manager took a senior executive on a day trip to experience what his life was like; this involved a 6am flight in economy (the cheapest option) and a ban on looking at e-mails during the flight or in the taxi because the company decreed that the network would not be secure.

Most of these frustrations are suffered by junior or middle managers. They are coping with rules set by those in the "c-suite", the chief executive, chief financial officer. For those chiefs, life is quite different, as the next chapter will explore.

6

THE CULT OF THE CHIEF EXECUTIVE

Sometimes, the very worst kind of manager is the person in charge of the company. John Preston's biography of Robert Maxwell, the late publishing tycoon, contains many anecdotes about how the old rogue used to humiliate his staff. Once he called Peter Jay, the economics journalist and former British ambassador whom he had hired as a "chief of staff", at 4am on a Saturday morning merely to ask him what time it was. At a business dinner, the editor of the *Daily Mirror* newspaper turned around only to find Maxwell helping himself to the food on his (the editor's) plate. If Captain Bob (as he was known) was dissatisfied with his meal, he would sometimes sweep the plate on to the floor and leave the servants to clear things up. And he thought nothing of bugging the phones of his staff and listening to their conversations.[1]

It is hard not to be reminded of the court of Louis XIV, the "Sun King" of France, who intercepted his courtiers' mail and had elaborate rules of etiquette, such as forbidding anyone from knocking on his door or sitting on a chair in his presence.[2] Like the French King, Maxwell enjoyed lavish spending and thrusting his name into the limelight at every opportunity. At one point, Maxwell even hired trumpet-playing heralds to announce his arrival at a party.

Over the years, experienced investors and auditors have developed warning signs of corporate excess. Three of the triggers are a fountain in the entrance area, a picture in the annual report of the chairman stepping out of a helicopter and a boss who is involved in a football club. Maxwell was fond of helicopters and became involved at both Oxford United and Derby County (where the supporters used to sing: "He's fat, he's round, he's never at the ground.") These alarm bells indicate to investors that executives are far more interested in the trappings of wealth than in genuinely growing the business.

Maxwell's financial problems emerged as a result of his egotism; he was inclined to overpay for businesses to steal a march on his rival, Rupert Murdoch. When Maxwell died, it was revealed he had been siphoning money from the company's pension funds to pay off the business's debts. He is now remembered not as a swashbuckling businessman, but as a fraudster.

Despite the example of Maxwell, many commentators seem to treat the wealthiest plutocrats with the same reverence we once gave to absolute monarchs. In the TV show *The Apprentice*, Donald Trump (in the USA) and Lord Sugar (in Britain) were portrayed as powerful potentates, with the contestants forced to undertake tasks to earn their favour and avoid elimination. Each week, one contestant was told "You're fired" like a medieval courtier condemned to exile. The irony is that neither Trump nor Sugar are representative of the corporate elite; the people who run the big multinationals have better things to do than appear on a game show.

Trump's spell on the show helped propel his rise to the presidency. If he could be smart enough to make billions in business, people reasoned, he must be smart enough to run the country. (His actual business record is extremely chequered.) His business background seemed to put him in a different class from professional politicians who, voters assumed, were only in it for themselves.

The elevation of corporate bosses represented a shift in attitude. Previously when US voters looked for an outsider, they chose generals, such as Dwight Eisenhower and Ulysses Grant, to be their president. The elevation of Trump was part of a trend. His cabinet was estimated as one of the wealthiest in history and included Rex Tillerson, the former head of oil giant ExxonMobil, and Wilbur Ross, a private-equity veteran. Michael Bloomberg, who made his billions supplying information to the financial sector, was mayor of New York for 11 years and ran for president. Silvio Berlusconi, a media tycoon, was prime minister of Italy for nine years.

In general, rich executives are celebrated in a cult-like manner. We revere them because they make lots of money and we tend to think that their wealth qualifies them to speak on a wide range of subjects. When Elon Musk, the founder of Tesla, tweets about a cryptocurrency, he can make the price move dramatically; if he is smart enough to develop an electric car, some investors reckon, he must be smart enough to foretell market movements. Musk, Jeff Bezos, the founder of Amazon, and Richard Branson of Virgin have all set up space programmes, making them the 21st-century equivalents of

King Ferdinand and Queen Isabella of Spain, who financed Columbus's expedition to the New World.

Of course, just as powerful executives are heroes to some, they are villains to others. During the pandemic, ridiculous conspiracy theories spread about the role of Bill Gates, the Microsoft founder, in developing vaccines through his charitable foundation. Like a Bond villain, corporate titans are assumed to be so influential they control everything that is going on in the world.

The bucks stop here

The existence of ultra-wealthy executives is a relatively modern phenomenon. There were some extremely powerful businessmen in the late 19th century such as John Rockefeller and Andrew Carnegie, but these were people who founded and controlled big companies. In the 20th century, ownership became separated from management; most large companies were run by hired hands rather than the original founders. This reduced executive rewards. In 1965, the average US chief executive earned 20 times as much as the average worker, according to the Economic Policy Institute, a think-tank. Then things switched again; by 2018, this ratio was 278 times. Put another way, between 1978 and 2018, US CEO pay rose 1,000% in real terms, whereas workers' pay rose just 12%.[3] Unless you think executives suddenly started being ten times more productive, something funny has been going on.

In part, these outsize gains stem from a change in philosophy in the 1970s and 1980s. Back then, chief executive pay was nowhere near as high as it is today but shareholders feared that managers were obsessed with their own perks (cars, first-class flights, plush offices) rather than delivering high returns for investors. As a result, it was decided to reward managers with share options (giving them the right to buy stock at a set price) on the grounds that this would align their interest with those of shareholders. These options were awarded on top of executive pay packages and were a one-way bet for the managers concerned; if they expired worthless, the bosses had lost nothing but if they paid off, the returns were huge. By coincidence, this shift was followed by a long bull market in which share prices soared; investors prospered but executives did even better.

This is in contrast with Japan, where executive pay is a little more than a tenth of the US level and around a quarter of that received by British bosses. In part, the difference is due to a more egalitarian mindset but it is also because Japanese bosses have rarely been given share options; in any case, Japan's stock market has never recovered from the bursting of the 1980s bubble. Despite the lower pay, running a big Japanese company must be just as difficult as running a US or British multinational.

The second reason for the high salaries in the US is that boards started to use consultants to advise them. The consultants duly did their research and calculated the average level of chief executive pay. Ambitious boards, which wanted to recruit the best managers, then aimed at attracting the best bosses by paying above the average. After all, who wants to hire a below-average executive? Slowly but surely, the effect was to ratchet up executive pay levels across the corporate sector.

The final factor was the existence of a few companies,

mainly in the tech sector, where the founders had been able to hold on to big slices of the equity. Many of these companies have earned very high profits, relative to the amount of capital they need. These firms have grown extremely rapidly and have come to dominate their market niches, just as Rockefeller's Standard Oil did in the 19th century. When the firms floated on the stock market, these founders (like Jeff Bezos of Amazon and Mark Zuckerberg of Facebook) became enormously wealthy, as did many of their fellow executives. Their success forced up salaries across the tech sector.

Top executives travel on private jets, or in the first-class cabins of airlines, where curtains are drawn to keep them out of sight of the hoi polloi. On land, they are ferried around by chauffeurs in fancy cars and dine at the most prestigious restaurants. If they have founded their own firms, they may well face the same dynastic issues as monarchs, struggling to decide which of their children is qualified to succeed them.

Magazines often write breathless profiles about the managers and their lifestyles, extolling their work habits. They get up early to send e-mails. They go to the gym. They attend charity dinners. Few pieces focus on the people who must answer the e-mails, drive them to the gym or serve the food at the dinners; it is as if executives operate in a vacuum.

What especially irritates about these examples is that they imply that the wealth of executives is justified by their long hours. But if time spent at work were the key criterion, people who hold down two jobs, or work overnight shifts in hospitals, would be rolling in money. It is also annoying to read about the executive's exercise routines. This does not necessarily translate into management skill. Winston

Churchill ran the British war effort on a diet of cigars, brandy and afternoon naps.

Given all this money and adulation, it is not surprising that some chief executives develop a high opinion of themselves. Some people have used the "psychopath test", developed by Bob Hare, a Canadian psychologist, to conclude that many corporate bosses fit the bill. Among the qualities that denote a psychopath are superficial charm, a grandiose sense of self-worth and a lack of empathy. One researcher found that between 3% and 21% of chief executives could be classed as psychopaths, compared with just 1% of the general population.[4] It is easy to see why people get the impression of callousness, when companies that fire workers tend to see a big rise in their share prices.

Bartleby has met a fair number of executives over the years, and his impression is that the vast majority are very hard-working (and serious) people who are conscious of their great responsibilities. Mind you, most executives will tend to be on their best behaviour in the presence of journalists. There are undoubtedly fashions in management as there are in other areas of life. In the 21st century, there has tended to be a shift away from the hard-charging style of Jack Welch, the former boss of General Electric, to a more socially conscious approach, exemplified by Paul Polman, the former head of Unilever.

Still, many readers will be aware of quite a few executives who meet the "grandiose sense of self-worth" criterion. This is particularly true of those who founded their companies. There is a tendency (admittedly, mostly in the US) to create a cult of the entrepreneur, seeing them as the modern equivalent of the warrior-king or great explorer, conquering new territory and advancing the cause of civilisation. But it is worth remembering that lots of entrepreneurs work hard and have good ideas. Despite their hard work, most fail, perhaps because their timing isn't right or because sufficient funding isn't available. In his book *Thinking, Fast and Slow*, psychologist Daniel Kahneman writes that his favourite equations are "success = talent + luck and great success = a little more talent and a lot more luck".[5]

Some chief executives are, indeed, exceptionally talented. But even a pioneer like Steve Jobs at Apple was not solely responsible for the group's success (he was forced out of the company at one point when it struggled to follow up the success of the Mac computer). Jonathan Ive, the chief design officer, played a vital role in the look of the iPhone and the iPad.

In most companies, the chief executive may make the big strategic decisions but cannot possibly claim credit for everything that goes right in the business. Some success is down to the health of the economy or the failed strategies of their competitors; a lot is due to the efforts of ordinary staff. Indeed, top executives often try to deny responsibility when things go wrong. When Jeffrey Skilling, the former chief executive of failed energy company Enron, was quizzed about the financing methods it used, he said: "I'm not an accountant."[6] Given that Mr Skilling received remuneration of $132m at Enron's peak, his claim of ignorance was striking. He was eventually sent to prison for securities fraud and other issues.

The problem with executive pay is that, at least in the

last 40 years, it always seems to go up, regardless of the economic circumstances. Take the pandemic of 2020. Life wasn't easy for hotel chains or cruise lines. But Christopher Nassetta, the chief executive of Hilton, received an 161% pay rise and Frank Del Rio of Norwegian Cruise Lines more than doubled his compensation to $36m, even though both firms lost money. It helped that both executives were awarded extra grants of shares after the downturn hurt their previous option packages.[7] At other firms, results were adjusted to omit bad quarters so executives could meet bonus targets. Heads they win, tails they win.

Indeed, pay growth far outstripped performance. Between 2000 and 2013, the pay of chief executives at leading British companies rose by 350%, while pre-tax profits rose by 195% and revenues by 140%.[8] Another problem with the structure of executive pay is that it encourages a focus on the short term; making sure the company meets the profits for the next quarter rather than focusing on long-term investment. A study by FCLT Global found that the average duration of executive compensation plans was just 1.7 years.[9]

One argument in favour of higher pay is that executives are subject to the same "war for talent" that has caused footballers to move all over the world in search of big pay cheques; the likes of Neymar and Kylian Mbappe are much sought after. But executive recruitment is nothing like as international as football; a 2013 study of Fortune 500 companies showed that less than 1% had hired a chief executive from abroad. A rather better argument is that executives can move to work for companies that are not quoted on the stock market, where their pay does not have to be publicly disclosed. These businesses are funded by private equity investors, who are willing to pay for managers who they believe can outperform.

Shareholders seem not to have bothered too much about these pay packages. In part, no doubt, this was because most shares are owned by big institutional investors, whose own executives are extremely well paid. Hedge funds, which charge big fees because they promise to generate good returns in all kinds of market conditions, are the richest of the bunch. In 2020, 15 hedge fund managers made more than $1bn each.[10] These managers benefit from performance fees that pay off handsomely if things go well; if the manager looks after $5bn and assets rise 20% in the following year, a 2% performance fee would be $20m. Making money from managing other people's money has been one of the surest ways to rapid wealth.

Indifference to high pay is also a question of scale. The average market value of a company in the S&P 500 index in early 2021 was $60bn. Compared with that, the mean chief executive pay of $15–20m was pretty tiny; not enough to affect returns. There was the occasional investor revolt when a particular group of executives pushed things too far. In early 2021, six leading US companies, including GE and IBM, failed to win shareholder support for pay packages.[11] But even where shareholders do object, their votes on pay are purely advisory; boards can just ignore them. This makes a nonsense of the idea that businesses are run for the benefit of investors. One suspects that some executives regard shareholders rather like the old adage about children: they should be seen but not heard.

High executive pay has played its part in exacerbating the trend towards inequality that has been seen in many western nations in recent decades. It is different from the era of 100 years ago when most rich people were the beneficiaries of inherited wealth; today's rich have mostly worked hard for a living. But these executives are accumulating wealth, as well as income, which means it will be passed on to future generations; we are creating a new hereditary elite.

7

MODERN MANAGERS

Good management matters. Gallup estimates that the cost of poor management and lost productivity from disengaged employees amounts to between $960bn and $1.2trn a year.[1] Globally, the Gallup survey found that just 15% of employees were engaged with their business, although 34% felt that way in the US. Companies with better employee engagement had lower absenteeism and job turnover, higher customer ratings, productivity and profitability.[2]

In businesses where employees need to use their judgment and creativity, workers need to feel their efforts are appreciated. Often the tone is set by the top. The quirks of a powerful chief executive are transmitted through a company, from their approach to conducting meetings, through the language they use in memos, to the way they dress and treat their subordinates. If the big boss is a bully, the junior managers are more likely to be bullies as well. The stated values of ride-hailing company Uber included such messages as "champion's mindset" and "always be hustlin'". The result was a hard-charging culture which may have helped the company grow quickly but eventually led to a series of scandals and the departure of Travis Kalanick, Uber's founder.

An aggressive culture manifests itself in the bullying of junior staff. Acas, the British conciliation service, says that bullying occurs when workers are "frightened, less respected or put down, made fun of or upset"; examples include being put down regularly in meetings or being given heavier workloads than colleagues. Often, the result is that people leave the company to escape the hostility; sometimes the bullying is so bad that they can sue for compensation (although such deals are often covered up by non-disclosure agreements). Around 13% of German employees have been bullied by their boss, according to an academic study, and this can be extremely stressful.[3]

The effect is to create a toxic workplace. In his book *Toxic*, Clive Lewis writes that such workplaces can involve "colleagues who feel no requirement to moderate their behaviour" and "line managers who are preoccupied with status and power rather than organisation objectives".[4] In the past, workers might have been expected to put up with this but there is a growing recognition that such behaviour is not just unfair; it is inefficient and sometimes illegal.

Toxicity is only one example of what people refer to when they talk about "corporate culture". The term dates back to the early 1980s when authors Tom Peters and Robert Waterman cited culture as one of the key ingredients of successful businesses in their book *In Search of Excellence*.[5] In an ideal world, employees are so steeped in the corporate ethos that they know the right thing to do in any situation, without reading a memo or checking in with their boss.

In the right culture, employees can take the initiative; giving a discount to a long-term customer to keep their business, for example. But in the wrong culture, employees are too frightened to do anything of the sort because they fear that they will be punished for breaking the rules. Robert Maxwell was famous for his temper, often blaming other people for his own mistakes. It was hardly surprising that no subordinate was able to stop his mismanagement.

Psychological safety

A dictatorial approach leads to lots of problems as Amy Edmondson, a professor at Harvard Business School, pointed out in her book *The Fearless Organisation*.[6] She cites a couple of tragic examples. In 1977, two Boeing 747s crashed in the Canary Islands when a co-pilot felt unable to query his captain's decision to take off, after the captain had misunderstood the instructions from air-traffic control. And in 2003, an engineer on the Columbia space shuttle programme saw the risk of damage to the vehicle's wing but felt unable to speak as he was too low down the hierarchy at NASA.

There are plenty of other examples in less life-threatening circumstances. Ms Edmondson points to Volkswagen, which was caught up in a scandal over its attempts to manipulate the results of tests for diesel emissions. The company's culture was based on intimidation; on one occasion, engineers were threatened with dismissal if they failed to improve a model's bodywork within six weeks. The problem with such cultures is that they may appear to be successful in the short term, but in the long run employees will be tempted to cover up any problems, or use subterfuge to get round them.

Creating an atmosphere of "psychological safety", as Ms Edmondson recommends, means that workers can speak their minds without fear of reprisal. This is not just a matter of being "nice"; it may include the need to rubbish a colleague's idea if it is ill-considered. But in the right culture, workers should be able to take such criticism on the chin, provided it is aimed at the idea, not the person.

In contrast, a personnel approach that was briefly popular in the US corporate sector was called "rank and yank"; each year, the employees would be rated against each other, with those at the bottom of the rankings facing dismissal. This approach was most associated with Jack Welch, the aggressive head of GE, the conglomerate. Welch was nicknamed "Neutron Jack" for his tendency to lay people off, after the neutron bomb that killed people but left buildings still standing. He believed that candid appraisal of employees was essential. "We grade children in school, often as young as 9 or 10, and no one calls that cruel," he told the *Wall Street Journal*. "But somehow adults can't take it? Explain that one to me."[7]

The inherent flaw of ranking systems is that businesses depend on employees co-operating with one another. If employee A needs help on a project, then employees B and C may be disinclined to help if they know that the result is that A keeps her job at the expense of their own.

To test the point, Jan Woike, from the Max Planck Institute in Berlin, and Sebastian Hafenbrädl, of the IESE business school in Barcelona, devised a game which involved participants being given tokens to invest.[8] Contestants could either invest in an individual project or collectively. Two different forms of the game were played. In both, the eventual returns were higher if everyone collaborated. But in one version, investing in the individual project improved the participant's relative ranking, even though the returns (for both the individual and the group) were lower.

In the relative ranking version of the game, individuals were told how well they scored and how well they were performing compared with the rest of the group. In another, they were informed about how well the group as a whole was performing, relative to the maximum possible return. The second approach led to more co-operation. In the first version, players were inclined to focus on their individual ranking, even though the returns would be lower. The authors concluded: "Ranking feedback, which is often used in organisational settings, prompts people to perceive even situations with co-operative outcome structures as competitive."

The academics are too kind. Working at any company that sets employees to compete against each other sounds not just "competitive" but deeply unpleasant. There is a reason why the salesmen in *Glengarry Glen Ross*, the David Mamet play, turn to robbing the business in an attempt to avoid the sack; desperation can bring out the worst in people.

Ethical standards at companies also depend on how employees are treated. If people who bend the rules get promoted and those who behave ethically do not, more rule-breaking will occur. A paper by academics at Columbia and Harvard universities looked at how companies could reduce unethical behaviour within their ranks.[9] The paper found that employees were more likely to lie, or commit fraud, when they were set really challenging goals. Research also shows that people are more likely to behave well if potential ethical questions are raised before they start the task; for example, those who signed an ethics code were more likely to report their car mileage accurately.

Feedback

One of the ways in which managers can improve their relations with staff is through the way they conduct formal processes. Chapter 1 discussed how interview techniques are subject to bias on a wide number of grounds. Many of the same problems occur with the way that employees' performance is assessed and how they are given feedback.

The first problem is that the format is too rigid, often in the form of a formal annual review. All too often this is a stale, box-ticking exercise. Although it is necessary to let workers know how they are performing, the process needs to be continuous and informal. Cramming everything into one session, after a 12-month delay, is a mistake.

Indeed, it is foolish to rely on an occasional approach whether the feedback is good or bad. If the employee is performing well, timely positive feedback will encourage them to keep doing so. If the employee is performing badly, waiting several months to tell them is not good for either the company or the worker.

A Gallup survey found that 47% of employees received feedback from their managers "a few times or less" a year.[10] Perhaps that doesn't matter because only 26% of employees "strongly agreed" that the feedback helped them work better. Strikingly, only 34% of workers strongly agreed that their managers knew what projects they were working on.

There is also a tendency for the manager who undertakes the review to go through the motions. Note will be taken of the training courses the employee has attended and goals (which can seem entirely arbitrary) will be set for the following year. Unlike the interview process, feedback should not be too standardised. A set list of questions may be fine when the company knows little about the outside candidates. Once the employee has spent time at the company, feedback should be tailored to their individual needs and experiences.

Although the discussion may be idiosyncratic, managers should be very clear as to how employees are being judged. As three Stanford academics have observed: "Ambiguity in the criteria used to evaluate employees leads to biased outcomes," adding that "be innovative" is a rather woolly instruction.[11] The manager should prepare a checklist of criteria (of which the employees should be aware) so they can ensure that workers are judged consistently.

Giving feedback to employees is a tricky element of a manager's life; there is a fine line to be drawn between complete honesty and the risk of causing offence or undermining morale. It is important to avoid the kind of adjectives that have negative connotations when applied to certain groups: "strident" or "shrill" tend to be used only for women whereas men are described as "forthright".

The discussion should not be one-way. A feedback session should be the moment when the employee has the chance to raise any issues that they have been unable to air during the working day. In some cases, companies have adopted a "360 degree" appraisal system in which workers rate managers as well as the other way round. It is a neat idea but works better in theory than in practice. Even when the company promises that the process is anonymous, workers will hesitate to badmouth the boss. Whether or not the worker trusts the company to keep its word, there is always the risk that the specifics of the complaint can be used to identify the individual concerned.

Although it seems obvious that giving employees feedback should be essential to their performance, it doesn't always work. A meta-study in 2000 found that, despite a positive effect on average, feedback worsened employee performance in 38% of cases.[12] The authors suggest that feedback works best when it concerns how specific tasks are performed and works badly if it focuses on an individual's personality.

Another problem is that feedback is too limited; it could be used by managers to give workers a better idea of what the organisation is trying to do. The Gallup survey found that only 41% of US employees strongly agreed that they knew what their organisation stood for, or what made it different from its competitors. Globally, only 50% of employees knew what was expected from them at work.[13]

The gentle touch

Perhaps the template for the tough manager dates back to the early days of the industrial revolution. The first factory workers had spent their lives working either as artisans or farm workers, where they had some control over either the hours or the pace at which they worked. Factory owners had invested a lot of money in machinery and they wanted to get the maximum return. As a result, they insisted on strict discipline. Indeed, many factory owners preferred to hire women, or children, who were easier to control.

The harsh rule of managers (and their agent, the factory foreman) explains why workers decided to form trade unions so they could fight to get better pay and working conditions. One industry that was plagued by industrial disputes was car manufacturing, and the result was often poor quality cars produced at high prices. Consumers had to put up with the situation because the industry was dominated by a few producers, such as General Motors, Ford and Chrysler in the US or British Leyland in the UK. But in the 1970s, strong competition emerged in the form of the Japanese producers which initially focused on smaller, cheaper vehicles. The pioneer was Toyota, which had developed a "lean manufacturing system" designed to reduce waste and eliminate faults. A key element was a concept called *jidoka*, which means "automation with a human touch".[14] Any workers could stop the production line to prevent a fault. This required management to trust the workers to make responsible decisions, and implied a much more collaborative approach than the western system.

More generally, treating employees well seems to work. Alex Edmans of the London Business School conducted a study looking at those businesses ranked the "100 best companies to work for" published by *Fortune* magazine. The data (compiled by the Great Place to Work Institute) cover the period 1984 to 2011. After controlling for factors such as size and industry sector, the businesses that treated their staff well produced stock-market outperformance of 2.3–3.8% a year, a substantial cumulative gain.[15]

In his book *The Art of Fairness*, David Bodanis recounts a

number of tales about managers who have had striking success by treating their workers with fairness and empathy.[16] One of the most striking examples is the Empire State Building, which was built in just 13 months in the 1930s, a period which also included the dismantling of the hotel that originally occupied the site. Paul Starratt, the builder, paid his workers double the daily rate and devoted a lot of attention to safety, paying the employees in full on days when it was too windy to operate. Hot meals were delivered to the workers, even on the higher floors. The project had very low staff turnover and workers even suggested productivity improvements.

Another example cited by Mr Bodanis was from the public sector; the 2012 London Olympics opening ceremony organised by Danny Boyle, the film director. Thousands of volunteers were needed for the ceremony but that created the risk that the details would leak. Rather than make the volunteers sign a legal non-disclosure agreement (the conventional approach), Mr Boyle trusted them to keep the secret. The volunteers lived up to their part of the deal, partly because Mr Boyle treated them in a grown-up fashion, listening to their suggestions and ensuring they were paid for their costumes.

By and large, the services sector requires a collaborative approach between workers and managers. If the job requires any kind of creativity, or use of initiative, it is fruitless to attempt to turn the workers into automatons. An interesting example is Timpsons, the British high-street chain that specialises in key cutting and shoe repair. Sir John Timpson, the founder, believes in "upside down management" which involves trusting the staff to serve the customers in any way they want. They are allowed to change prices and settle disputes. The main two rules are "look the part" and "put the money in the till".

Of course, there will always be workers who will take advantage of employers and "swing the lead". (This metaphor comes from the days when sailors used a piece of lead on a line to check the water depth; lazy mariners would simply swing the lead in the air rather than dip it in the ocean.) In a services-based economy, checking a worker's productivity is less easy than it used to be; managers cannot count how many widgets they have produced or bricks they have laid.

In some parts of the economy, it can be impossible to improve productivity. An economist called William Baumol described this problem; it takes the same number of musicians the same amount of time to play a Schubert string quartet as it did when the piece was first produced.[17] But despite this lack of productivity improvements, musicians' wages have risen in real terms over the centuries. That is because those who employ musicians need to offer a wage sufficient to deter them from taking a job as, say, a plumber or a teacher. In a sense, workers in low productivity sectors "free ride" on the back of improvements in more competitive industries.

Coaching

As this chapter has made clear, managing people is not an easy task. Even those who have reached the top of the greasy pole can benefit from outside advice. Three top Google executives – Eric Schmidt, Jonathan Rosenberg and Alan Eagle – wrote a book in tribute to a man who advised them, Bill Campbell.[18] Campbell was originally a college coach of American football before working at Apple, heading the marketing campaign for the original Macintosh, and then becoming chief executive at Intuit, a financial software company. But in the later stages of his career, he acted as an executive coach to businesses funded by venture capital firm Kleiner Perkins; he was a board member of Apple and advised executives at Google, eBay, Facebook and Twitter. In 2000, he told the board of Amazon not to replace Jeff Bezos as chief executive, a suggestion that proved very wise in retrospect.

Campbell believed that managers need to be honest, humble and willing to learn. His philosophy was: "Your title makes you a manager, your people make you a leader." He was willing to make sharp criticisms of those he coached but in private, not in public. Mr Campbell died in 2016 but the idea of the manager as a coach lives on; the aim of a business manager, as in sport, is to get the best out of their team.

Real-world sporting coaches can also be seen as role models for the modern corporate manager. A classic example is Gareth Southgate, who in 2021 guided the England football team to its first major final in 55 years. Southgate is typical of many chief executives in that he rose through the ranks; a former England player, he coached the under-21 national team from 2013 to 2016. He was thus familiar with many of the team's players and they were used to his style.

It is easy to imagine Southgate as, say, a regional manager of Unilever. He dresses formally, wearing a three-piece suit during the 2018 World Cup and speaking carefully and thoughtfully during interviews. He is noted for his meticulous preparation, carefully studying the teams that England will face and the potential weaknesses of individual opponents. On another occasion, he organised breathing lessons so the team could reduce their tension after a stressful game.[19] In style, he was the calm adviser rather than the rigid martinet. He is also extremely inclusive, going out of his way to praise some of the reserve members of the squad for their efforts in helping to keep the team ready for action.

But this approach doesn't stop him from being ruthless when he needs to be. One of his first acts as manager was to drop Wayne Rooney, the team's ageing talisman, and he later suspended players (including Raheem Sterling, one of the stars of the 2021 tournament) for breaches of discipline. In 2021, he twice substituted players who had themselves come on as substitutes, often seen as a sharp rebuke.

Finally, Southgate could easily be a representative of the new socially conscious breed of corporate manager. He supported his players when they took the knee to protest against racism and wrote a letter to England fans, stating that it was the duty of players "to continue to interact with the public on matters such as equality, inclusivity and racial injustice, while using the power of their voices to help put debates on the table, raise awareness and educate."[20]

Survival of the fittest?

The idea of the manager as coach is a counterweight to the long-running tendency to treat business as a Darwinian struggle to succeed, in which selfishness is essential. In fiction, this was famously represented by the character Gordon Gekko in the film *Wall Street*, who said not just that "greed is good" but: "Greed clarifies, cuts through, and captures the essence of the evolutionary spirit."

In theory, intense competition is good for consumers

and the economy; it keeps prices low and enhances efficiency. But it is remarkable how many executives dislike competition and try to avoid it. The big technology companies that have emerged in the 21st century dominate their sectors; Amazon in online shopping, Google in internet search and Facebook in social networks, for example. When new competitors emerge, the tech giants have the capital to buy them up before they become a serious threat.

Regulators have to keep a constant watch to ensure that companies do not combine to keep prices, or profit margins, high. Adam Smith, the pioneer of political economics, noted this in his 1776 book *The Wealth of Nations* when he declared: "People of the same trade seldom meet together, even for merriment and diversion, but the conversation ends in a conspiracy against the public, or in some contrivance to raise prices."[21] Companies often lobby for tariffs on foreign goods, or quotas, to reduce competition.

Furthermore, businesses do not succeed on their own. They depend on suppliers, distributors and retailers, as well as a host of service providers from accounting through legal services to security. And all this depends on infrastructure provided by the public sector, such as roads, ports, courts and policing as well as the education system to train the workforce and the health service to keep employees well. Businesses also have an effect on the wider community whether in a positive sense (being the core employer that sustains a town) or a negative one (polluting the air or the water supply).

A growing recognition of these links has led to the growth of the sustainability movement, also known as ESG (yet another acronym; this one stands for environmental, social and governance). To quote Paul Polman, one of the leaders of the movement, the aim is "a business that improves well-being for everyone it impacts and at all scales – every product, every operation, every region and country, and for every stakeholder, including employees, suppliers, communities, customers, and even future generations and the planet itself".[22]

It is an ambitious aim, and proponents of ESG tend to get stick from both the left and the right. On the left, the suspicion is that the high ideals are just a smokescreen for the underlying aim of maximising profits. Mentioning environmental targets is dubbed "greenwashing", for example. On the right, the ideals are mocked as "woke capitalism"; Milton Friedman, the free-market economist, proclaimed that the duty of businesses was to serve their investors. The latter would generally want "to make as much money as possible while conforming to the basic rules of the society, both those embodied in law and those embodied in ethical custom".[23] To the extent that executives have social concerns, they should use their own money to finance them, not that of their shareholders; if the shareholders wish to reduce pollution or fight racism, they can do so with the money earned from their investments. In Mr Friedman's view, the two goals should not be confused.

There is something in both these criticisms. In August 2019, 181 US bosses in a club called the Business Roundtable signed a declaration in favour of stakeholder capitalism, under which companies engage with a wider range of groups than just their shareholders; employees, customers, suppliers and society in general. But despite the warm words, a study in

March 2020 found that very few of the companies involved had taken any practical steps since signing the document.[24] Furthermore, some companies produce grandiose mission statements such as "our mission is what drives us to do everything possible to expand human potential" (Nike) or "our purpose unifies us in a common cause and growth strategy of improving more consumers' lives in small but meaningful ways each day" (Procter & Gamble), which are very hard to tie down to specifics. Enron, the energy company that collapsed after its accounting approach was revealed to be flawed, cited "respect, integrity, communication and excellence" as its core values.[25]

Another problem is that the criteria for deciding which companies qualify as "good" under the ESG measure can be very woolly. An analysis by *The Economist* found little correlation between the scores achieved by companies under two leading ESG rating systems.[26]

Shareholders have the right to question whether executives who take political stances are doing so just to gain attention, and might be harming the business by alienating potential customers. The optimistic case is that it is possible to serve both shareholders and the broader society. A company that treats its employees badly is likely to falter in the long run; the same goes for a business with a tendency to pollute or that short-changes its suppliers. Young customers are willing to support brands that are linked to the social causes they support, and to boycott those that do not. A meta-study of academic reports that looked at the relationship between ESG portfolios and investment returns found that the approach did not tend to damage returns.[27] Wouldn't we rather companies tried to behave in a socially responsible fashion?

The optimistic case for modern management is that it is possible to treat employees well, and consider the wider impact on society of a company's actions, and be successful. Indeed, these qualities may be essential because treating employees badly or ignoring the societal effects of corporate decisions will eventually rebound on the business. Of course, there are plenty of people who will advise executives on being good managers and their influence is the subject of the next chapter.

8

HELPING HANDS

Small companies have to rely on their own resources. But large companies attract outside advisers in the same way that jam jars attract wasps. All of them are eager to help, and all are equally eager to take a fee. Senior staff will meet a lot of these would-be counsellors and junior staff will worry whenever they get involved with the firm's affairs. Bartleby's rule of hiring advisers is: *it is nearly always a better deal for the advisers than the advised.*

Call in the consultants
When a company is searching for ideas about how to improve its operations, it may take the well-worn step of calling in a team of management consultants. A bright young team of sharp-suited professionals will arrive (with a senior person in charge) to ask thousands of questions and will solemnly enter numbers into a host of spreadsheets.

It is easy to be cynical about management consultants, so let's go for it. The old joke about management consultants is that they borrow your watch so they can tell you the time, and then they walk off with the watch. The essence of their work is that their information comes from the client; it is only their analysis that is added value.

That raises the question of whether their expensive analysis is useful. After all, if these people really know exactly how to successfully run a business, shouldn't they do it themselves? The rewards would surely be greater as an entrepreneur than as a consultant. It is like the old jibe about teachers: "Those who can, do. Those who can't, teach."

When consultants' advice does come, the common criticism is that it is generic, and based around a blizzard of jargon or acronyms. An example is SWOT analysis, which stands for strengths, weaknesses, opportunities and threats. It is a reasonable way of thinking about a business, but it may only point out obvious problems, rather than offer solutions. When asked to outrace Usain Bolt, normal folk may understand their weakness (they are not fast enough) but the sharpest minds will be unable to help them overcome it.

To inspire their clients, consultants may refer to the success of well-known companies like Toyota (and its total quality management), but such paragons have developed their strengths over long periods. Other companies will struggle to imitate these shining examples. Furthermore, management advice tends to have fashions; in one period, consultants will emphasise the importance of focusing on a core business; in another, on the virtues of diversification.

But an obvious rebuttal to this generic criticism is that, if the advice of consultants is useless, why are so many companies willing to pay for it? Global business revenues for management consultants were estimated at $160bn in

2019 (up from $107bn in 2011).[1] However, it is very hard to measure how effective this advice turns out to be. One survey indicates that fewer than half of clients believe the advice they receive is consistently worth more than the fees.[2] There is not a lot of independent research into the issue. A study by the World Bank and Stanford University of the Indian textile industry found significant gains (an 80% return on capital) for firms that hired consultants.[3] But this may have been an example of "catch-up" where modern ideas were brought to a set of family-owned businesses. The same effects might not be achievable in a large multinational. The main motivation for hiring consultancies may be that executives in difficulty look for help wherever they can find it in the belief that, at the very least, a fresh perspective will be useful.

By virtue of their wide range of clients, management consultants also have the opportunity to observe how business practices are changing, and many report on these trends in their research. This information is highly useful for those outside observers (politicians, consumer groups, journalists) who want to know how businesses are adapting to new situations. Consultants may also play a role in spreading best practice throughout the sectors they cover. Whether this justifies their fees is another matter. Their role brings to mind the quote from John Wanamaker, an American retail tycoon in the early 20th century: "Half the money I spend on advertising is wasted: the trouble is I don't know which half." Advice from management consultants could be useful but you won't find out till you pay them.

The bankers

All businesses, even small ones, need some kind of relationship with a banker. Historically the main criticism of banks is that they are inconsistent in their lending approaches. When the economy is booming, they are eager to lend as much as possible, but at the first sign of trouble they close their chequebooks and even ask for loans to be repaid. The result can be that the business collapses. The old quip is that bankers will lend you an umbrella when the sun is shining but take it back when it's raining.

But the bankers that most workers really need to worry about inhabit skyscrapers, not branch offices. They are usually called "investment bankers" and they work for the giants of Wall Street, like Goldman Sachs and Morgan Stanley, or European behemoths such as UBS and Deutsche Bank. These banks don't earn their profits by lending money but by earning fees for arranging deals. The most aggressive of the breed work in mergers and acquisitions (M&A).

Warren Buffett, one of history's most successful investors, once quipped that a barber is the last person you should ask whether you need a haircut. By the same token, M&A professionals are unlikely to recommend that a company doesn't do a deal. In their view, you must either eat or be eaten; you are predator or prey. So they may suggest that a company raises money, or issues shares, to buy another business. They can cite a host of reasons for doing so; the target has a product or a technology that will be an exciting addition, it offers an opening into new countries or, most often, that there are "synergies" to be obtained by putting the two companies together.

In practice, synergies is a fancy word for cost cuts; money can be saved by reducing administrative expenses or by eliminating the need for some middle managers or staff in any division. That is one reason why workers should beware when investment bankers turn up. (Indeed, sometimes companies pursue a cost-cutting acquisition when they can think of no other way to increase their profits.) Another problem is that, even when workers don't lose their jobs, mergers cause a lot of disruption and anxiety; they often involve changes in the way businesses work, such as the management structure or the corporate culture.

Acquisitions are subject to the "winner's curse", which is also associated with auctions. To win an auction, buyers must be willing to pay a higher price than anyone else. In turn, this means they are valuing the object (or company) more highly than the consensus. This probably means they are overpaying. The predator company may have to take on lots of debt to buy the target, and that may weigh down the entire company for years.

As a result, many mergers and acquisitions don't deliver the promised benefits. One of the most spectacular failures was the takeover of Time Warner, the media giant, by AOL, the internet portal, in early 2001. The deal set off many alarms; there was little business overlap between the two companies and the top management roles were split with Steve Case of AOL becoming chairman and Gerald Levin of Time Warner becoming chief executive (a sign that there would be no clear leadership). AOL shareholders ended up with 55% of the combined group even though it was a much smaller business; AOL's share price had been bid up to ridiculous heights in the dotcom boom. The whole thing was a disaster. In short order, the company announced massive losses. Both Case and Levin departed and eventually AOL was spun off from the combined company.

Spin-offs are another option that investment bankers might suggest. One theory is that the stock market will value the separate parts of the company more highly than when they are pushed together. Another argument is that the management of the spun-off division will have more freedom to pursue its goals, once released from the suffocating embrace of the parent company.

Observant readers might notice the contradiction. If there are huge advantages to be gained from spin-offs, surely mergers shouldn't be pursued in the first place. But here is the beauty of the process. Investment bankers get paid for their advice in putting two companies together and get paid again for pulling them apart. For them, it's a win-win scenario.

Public relations

As with management consultancy, there is a problem in defining the usefulness of public relations teams. Clearly, big companies have to find some way of communicating with the press and with the public. Some companies have in-house public relations teams; some employ external consultants; some use both. On top of this, big firms will have separate investor relations teams to deal with their largest shareholders.

Some PR activity is reactive. Rumours about a company's products, or the way it treats its staff or the environment, can spread very quickly. Somebody has to be available to issue a flat denial or put out a plausible explanation. As the old saying goes: "A lie can be halfway round the world before the truth has got its boots on."

But public relations teams also try to be strategic advisers. They want to shape the "narrative" about the company. If the firm is perceived to be struggling, they try to emphasise new products or a new management approach. If it has a bad environmental record, the PR team try to place stories about new approaches or products that cut carbon emissions, and so on. And there will be a lot of dialogue between PR advisers and senior management as the former try to understand what kind of message the latter are trying to impart.

It is easy to see, in theory, why the best public relations people might be extremely valuable. But it is much harder to measure this in practice. When it comes to advertising, one can calculate the sales growth of the product. But what is the criterion for measuring the success of a PR campaign? Public perception of the company? Number of favourable mentions in the press? The share price? Given the difficulty, it is not surprising that a survey in the *Journal of Public Relations Research* found that only a few practitioners conduct a formal evaluation of the effectiveness of their efforts.[4]

In practice, many PR companies try to show how hard they are working by sending out a blizzard of press releases. These don't just go to the national press. People who don't work for the media may be surprised to learn how many specialist publications exist, covering industries (like retailing or mining) or broader subjects like fashion. Take *Cranes Today*, which presumably has a very high readership, or *Spudman*, for those who need to know more about potatoes. Journalists from these publications will have plenty of detailed questions for companies in their sectors – about the opening of new stores, or demand for certain items – and it is far better for a PR team to field these queries than for managers to be distracted from their day-to-day tasks.

The problem is that a lot of this news is quite trivial and some PR companies employ a scattergun approach to distributing their releases. For journalists like Bartleby, the result can be a kind of "groundhog day" interaction with junior PR people that consists of the following process. Day 1: PR person sends e-mail about client. Day 2: PR person sends follow-up e-mail to check journalist received the missive from the previous day. Day 3: PR person calls the journalist to make absolutely certain that they are aware of the e-mail's existence. Day 4: PR person sends a new e-mail about the same client, and the process starts all over again.

Clearly, there are some smart PR people and they can be very useful when the company has a genuine message to impart, such as a new strategy or product line. A good PR person can hone the message and know which journalists and publications are worth talking to. But an awful lot of PR activity is a pointless attempt to generate stories that no one really wants to cover.

There is also a bit of the gravy train about the whole business. On many occasions, Bartleby has been invited to lunch in a fancy restaurant by some PR person to meet the client. It often seems that the client has no idea why the lunch is taking place, and little in the way of useful information is imparted. But everyone has had a nice lunch at the client's expense. More expensive versions of this process occur at sports events, or the theatre.

Furthermore, while many journalists moan about the demands of PR people, quite a lot of them join the industry in search of a higher salary. The journalism–PR nexus is its own ecosystem in which both parties suspect the other and the client ends up paying. In the end, although a good PR team can be useful for a company, it will be unsuccessful unless there is a good story to write. Get the business right and the PR story will largely look after itself.

Academics

What about management research? Shouldn't that provide some useful tips? Business schools and universities have thousands of academics who are conducting research and publishing papers about the practice of management, in part for the prestige and in part because a top academic can earn significant fees from writing books and advising corporate clients.

As with consultancy, however, the problem is that it is hard to find concrete examples of the successful application of management advice. This would be a surprise to the pioneers of management theory like Frederick Winslow Taylor who developed the concept of "scientific management". The trouble is that his methods were not always that scientific. Taylor conducted one of his first exercises at the Bethlehem Iron Company. He based his calculations on a small group of well-built Hungarian workers who, attempting to impress him, managed to shift 16.5 tons of iron in quick time. This was the equivalent of shifting 71 tons a day. Taylor rounded this up to 75 tons and then, assuming that such sustained effort by all workers was impossible, cut the number by 40%

to create a daily target of 45 tons. At best, this was a "back of the fag packet" calculation.[5]

Another famous study, in the 1920s, of Western Electric's Hawthorne Works factory in Illinois seemed to show that productivity improved if the managers paid attention to the workers. The study was initially designed to find out whether better lighting improved productivity, but it appeared to show that output went up whether the lights were brighter or dimmer; it was the change that seemed to motivate workers. Studies since then, however, have showed the flaws in the experiment. It was based on only five women (two of whom were replaced during the study) and the improvement in output was not measured consistently. Worse still, the lights were always changed on Sundays, so the productivity improvement occurred on Mondays. But (as is often the case in factories) productivity was always better on Mondays, whether or not the lights were changed. This was a "day of week" effect, not a lighting impact.[6]

Raymond Hubbard, a professor of marketing at Drake University in Iowa, concluded that management research had produced "an empirical literature consisting almost entirely of unverified, fragile results whose role in the development of cumulative knowledge is of the shakiest kind".[7] Studies have shown that large portions of management research contain inconsistencies or errors, or do not disclose enough data to allow independent verification of their findings.

Another problem (which afflicts scientific research in general) is that papers that find striking results are more likely to be published in leading journals and to attract the attention of the media. A paper that finds, say, that drinking a cup of tea improves productivity is much more likely to get publicity than a paper that found a hot beverage has no effect altogether. But statistical variance means that some apparent correlations may simply be down to chance (such as the link between margarine consumption and divorce rates in Maine).[8] If you are an academic trying to get your research publicised, that is not a possibility you are likely to emphasise.

As a result, when other academics try to replicate earlier studies, they often fail to do so. Perhaps it isn't surprising that Dennis Tourish argues that "most management research isn't really read by anyone outside a small coterie, least of all by practising managers".[9]

May buy advancement

The main reason for the existence of business schools is to offer a master's in business administration (or MBA) to eager young people who want to get ahead in life. The boom in management education started in the 1960s; by the 1980s and 1990s, bright graduates from all over the world were queueing to get into the top business schools. Many of these are based in the US at universities such as Harvard, Yale, Stanford, Berkeley and Chicago. But Europe also has some prestigious schools, such as Insead in France and the London Business School.

The benefits of a course don't just stem from the skills that the business schools teach, which naturally include a strong grounding in financial analysis, management studies and marketing. They come from the connections that people make with other students while they are attending. That was one reason why the pandemic was particularly damaging to the appeal of an MBA; you don't make lifelong friendships on Zoom.

One criticism of business schools is that they churn out identikit students with good technical skills but no imagination – MBA is said to stand for "mediocre but arrogant". In some people's eyes, MBA graduates have a spreadsheet mentality, focused on the numbers; others argue that real entrepreneurs would get on with starting a business, rather than studying the theory. Business schools are aware of these criticisms and try to broaden their curricula, with Harvard Business School introducing a compulsory first-year course on "leadership and corporate accountability". One of the more popular areas for students in recent years has been "social entrepreneurship", which often involves the creation of non-profit businesses designed to meet social needs, such as clean water or cheap power.

And the arts are not neglected. At Oxford's Saïd Business School, Bartleby sat through a delightful session, organised by an academic called Pegram Harrison, in which students attempted to conduct a choir singing "O clap your hands" by Orlando Gibbons. It was an excellent lesson in leadership as over-confident students attempted to lead the group, despite their lack of experience, without asking the expert singers what role they expected the conductor to perform. The right answer was to listen to the experts in the team, set the pace but then let the choir govern itself.

It is not just young people who take MBAs. The business schools earn a decent income from executive courses, where managers come for short stays to brush up their skills and catch up on the latest trends. They may also seize the opportunity to make contact with contemporaries who might eventually offer them a job; this is a networking opportunity as well as an educational option.

On the same grounds, the hope is that an MBA will land young budding executives a high-paying job, probably in finance, consultancy or technology. The average base salary for a graduate from one of the five US schools with the biggest earnings potential was \$139,000 in 2019.[10] But it is an expensive gamble. The full cost of a two-year course at a top US school is \$200,000 and that doesn't include the opportunity cost of not earning a salary during that period. If you spend all that money and don't get a good job, the main legacy of an expensive MBA will be lots of debt. As a result, and due to a less hospitable attitude towards immigrants, the popularity of US MBAs among international students has declined. The number of full-time MBA programmes in the US fell by nearly a tenth between 2014 and 2018, according to the Association to Advance Collegiate Schools of Business.[11]

Many international students are opting to take courses at home, particularly in Asia; in 2001, there were only two Asian schools in the top 100 of the FT's global rankings, but by 2021 there were 14. Graduates of the Indian Institute of Management enjoyed an average salary of \$192,000 within three years. Two Chinese programmes (Fudan and Tsinghua) each enabled workers to almost triple their salaries after graduation.[12]

As with elite universities, the top business schools bestow some of their prestige on graduates; if the candidate is good enough to be admitted to the school and complete the course, companies may well assume that they are highly talented.

This factor means that MBA programmes are unlikely to disappear. For those candidates who can afford the fees, MBA programmes can be a useful haven during economic downturns, when it is more difficult to find a job.

Unless, however, you are determined to take a role in senior management, one suspects that some more practical skills will be more useful for those who want to survive and prosper at work. Advanced computer skills, foreign languages, financial analysis; these attributes may instantly increase your employability without involving a vast monetary outlay, and can be fitted in around your current job.

Self-help

This book is devoted to those who want to survive work. But many people want not just to survive but to thrive. They want to get promoted, earn more pay and climb the greasy pole. They look for the magic formula for success and they hope that someone has written down the answer in a self-help book.

So they buy the kind of tomes that appear in airport bookshops and have titles like *How to Succeed in Business*, *The Secret of Management Success* or *The Top 10 Habits of High-Flying Executives*. These inspirational books follow in the footsteps of *How to Win Friends and Influence People*, written by Dale Carnegie back in 1936 and of Norman Vincent Peale, whose 1952 book *The Power of Positive Thinking* was an inspiration for Donald Trump.

The long-running success of these books shows that their commonsensical advice strikes a chord with the public. By and large, the principles of the Carnegie book are hard to fault: "Try honestly to see things from the other person's point of view," for example, or: "Talk about your own mistakes before criticising the other person." And Mr Peale is certainly right that a degree of optimism is very useful in business, given all the obstacles to success that people may face. Alas Mr Carnegie's belief that everybody loves the sound of their own name may be the reason why some Americans insist on using the other person's name in every sentence ("That's a very good point, Dave").

But the huge sales of these books have spawned too many imitators. It is unlikely that any book can offer a sure path to success. The chances are that a self-help book will fall into one of two categories. Either the advice will be general and verge on the platitudinous (work hard, think creatively etc.), or it will focus on a few specific examples of individual success which others will find it impossible to replicate. However much you study the lives of Steve Jobs or Bill Gates, the chances that you will establish a leading technology company are vanishingly small.

Studying the record of successful companies has its uses, as does examining a few failures. But it is probably most helpful for those in senior management, rather than for employees at the start of their careers. People have to work their way up the corporate ladder before they can make significant strategic decisions. Successful managers call on years of experience.

Sometimes books succeed because they appeal to managers rather than ambitious workers. The 1998 book *Who Moved My Cheese?* by Spencer Johnson was a parable about dealing with sudden change. Many copies were handed out to staff by businesses undergoing reorganisation. So much so that if you are given a copy of *Who Moved My Cheese?,* your next question is likely to be: "Who took my job?"

Some of the general advice in self-help books can be too culturally specific. Take networking, which is a particularly US enthusiasm. In Britain, people who network aggressively are likely to be seen as insincere and pushy. Conversely, the British tendency to use humour and self-deprecation can be lost on US listeners, who may take the latter at face value and assume the speaker has modest talents.

Sometimes self-help advice seems plain daft. Take the power stance. In the 2010s this pose was adopted by several British Conservative politicians; it involved standing with your legs far apart, as if play-acting a hoop in a croquet competition. A paper published in 2010 suggested this stance made its users seem more powerful and helped their self-assurance. The problem with the idea is that researchers tried to replicate the effect in 2015, in a study five times larger than the original; they found no effects at all.[13]

Many people would like to believe that some small change in their behaviour will bring them instant success. But it is hard to beat the basics: work hard; live up to your promises; listen carefully to your customers and colleagues and treat both with respect; make sure you research what is happening in your market. To which one might add the golden rule: "Don't be an asshole." Because this advice is so simple, it is hard to extend to book length and that is why so many self-help books are full of padding and platitudes. You can help yourself most by saving your money and not buying them.

- 9 -

THE FUTURE OF
WORK. PART 1

People tend to have an inconsistent attitude to work. Sometimes they worry that they have too much of it; sometimes that there is too little to go around. And the same is true of their attitude towards the future of work. On the one hand, they marvel at the ingenuity of labour-saving devices that will reduce the tedium of the working day; on the other, they fret that such devices will put too many people out of their jobs.

Some commentators have hoped that there might be a middle way. In an essay called "The economic possibilities for our grandchildren", written in 1930, John Maynard Keynes speculated that "the economic problem may be solved, or be at least within sight of solution, within a hundred years".[1] Humans would only need to take paid employment for three hours a day, 15 hours a week. Keynes himself was a very hard worker, writing books and papers, advising governments and managing money. But he was also an aesthete who had no problem occupying his spare hours in reading or appreciating culture.

Back in 1930, Keynes was well aware of the existence of the "idle rich"; those who had inherited their wealth and had no need for paid employment. But in the 21st century, the wealthiest people have tended to earn their money in finance, business or entertainment; in the Forbes list of wealthiest Americans, 70% are self-made – up from less than half in 1984.[2] It is the poor who suffer most from enforced idleness, either because they lack the opportunity or the capacity to work. Unlike Keynes, they lack the income to be involved with aesthetic pursuits.

Unemployment tends to be associated with poor physical and mental health. But the same is true of working too hard. Research from the World Health Organisation and the International Labour Organisation calculated that, in 2016, 745,000 people around the world died from either heart disease or a stroke as a result of working more than 55 hours a week.[3] Relative to working 35–40 hours a week, putting in more than 55 hours increased the chance of death by stroke by 35% and of heart attacks by 17%. Both the number of deaths caused by long hours, and the number of people working such hours, is increasing; in 2016, such hours were put in by 9% of the global workforce.

So this balance is hard to strike. The pandemic proved to be an experiment in that many people were placed on part-time working or on furlough schemes where the government subsidised their salaries. A paper by researchers at the Centre for Business Research at the University of Cambridge found that "people working reduced hours or being furloughed do not have poorer mental health".[4] It concluded that the threshold for good mental health was working just one day a week;

there was little extra psychological benefit from further days. This suggests that having any kind of employment makes people feel useful. Of course, few people can afford to work one day a week; nor, at present, could we enjoy the same standard of living if everyone tried to do so.

Balancing the need to earn a decent income with the desire to have a fulfilling job is difficult. Many people look back to a "golden age" of work from the 1950s to the 1970s when it was possible for "blue collar" workers to hold down a well-paying factory job and return in their cars to their wife and children every evening. But these rosy memories leave out a lot. Far from being happy, workers frequently resorted to strike action; between 1957 and 1985, the average number of British working days lost to industrial action was 8.3m a year. In contrast, between 1986 and 2018, the average number of days lost to strikes was less than 1m a year. Many women chafed at being at home in the 1950s and 1960s and welcomed the chance to go out to work when the labour market allowed them to do so; the proportion of British women who were employed rose by 20 percentage points between 1971 and 2020.

But blue collar workers are an endangered species. There has been a steady decline in well-paid manufacturing jobs since 1980. Ever since the decline began, the concern has been that capitalist economies may be able to create jobs, but too many of them are low-paid and insecure. Often governments have had to top up workers' incomes with social benefits to ensure they have a decent standard of living. And the rise in female employment can also be portrayed in a less positive light: women are working because their households need two incomes to survive. Those women who have been to university may be able to enjoy well-paid interesting jobs, but many women are struggling to juggle their childcare with shift work in hospitality, healthcare or cleaning.

In other words, it is not just a trade-off between paid work and unemployment. It is more of a matrix in which employees are struggling to find work that is well paid and interesting while having enough flexibility to allow for a personal life, but all too often having to settle for jobs that have none of those characteristics. People don't just want a job, they want a good job.

Tied up with this issue is the relationship between employer and employee. The traditional stereotype was that a worker joined a company to work full time at 18 or 21, and stayed with that business (or at most two or three others) until they retired at 60 or 65. But that pattern was never universal; plenty of people were self-employed or worked part time. As Sarah Kessler points out in her book *Gigged*, when Uber launched in 2009, nearly all taxi drivers were already self-employed, as were 50% of information technology workers and 70% of truck drivers.[5]

The covid-19 pandemic has thrown another ingredient into the mix; the location where people work has become a significant subject for debate. Ever since the early 1800s, workers have steadily been lured into cities to work in specific locations. But during the lockdowns, we learned that many people in the services sector could work quite efficiently from a remote location. It may take many decades for the implications to play out. This chapter will discuss the effect of automation, and the next will examine how the gig economy and the pandemic may interact.

The risks of automation

In 1589, William Lee invented a stocking-frame knitting machine that would replace the slow process of hand-knitting.[6] But when he applied to Queen Elizabeth I of England for a patent, he was refused. 'I have too much love for my poor people who obtain their bread by the employment of knitting to give my money to forward an invention that will tend to their ruin by depriving them of employment and thus making them beggars,' the great Queen said.[7] This was one of the earliest examples of the concern that technological improvement would lead to unemployment.

In the early 1800s, an English group known as the Luddites tried to fight automation by smashing textile machinery. History (and some violent action by the British government) swept them aside. Today, it is computers and artificial intelligence programmes that threaten to put humans out of their jobs. Instead of manufacturing jobs, services sector work is at risk.

It is possible to paint two widely differing pictures of the future of work. In the optimistic scenario, automation reduces the drudgery of many traditional activities (making work more pleasant) while an ageing population means that a smaller pool of workers can demand higher wages (making work more rewarding). In the pessimistic scenario, that same automation throws millions either out of work or into part-time low-paid jobs, while enriching only a small, technocratic elite.

In 2013, Michael Osborne and Carl Benedikt Frey of the Oxford Martin School published a paper that suggested 47% of US jobs were at risk of automation.[8] As they emphasised at the time, this was not a prediction, although it was treated as such by some commentators. Instead, the Oxford duo broke down occupations into a series of tasks to estimate what proportion of the job could be done by machine, and then set an AI programme to analyse the results. As they pointed out in a later article, this allowed them to predict that some professions (such as being a waiter) could be automated before this started to happen in the real world.[9]

Broadly speaking, their study bolstered the pessimistic case. The authors found that the workers most exposed to automation had, on average, lower incomes and lower levels of education than those who were less likely to be affected. The effects may also vary according to gender. For example, more than 3.5m Americans (mostly men) drive trucks or vans for a living, and are at risk from the adoption of driverless vehicles. However, women are less threatened by automation, largely because a higher proportion of them work in caring professions.

In his book *A World Without Work*, Daniel Susskind writes that "more and more tasks will fall to machines" with "an ever-shrinking set of tasks" left to humans.[10] Jobs will be available but they will not be sufficient to prevent mass unemployment. The plight of humans will be akin to that of horses, which lost their role to tractors during the first half of the 20th century.

But when will this happen? Rather confusingly, given his general thesis, Mr Susskind writes that "current fears about an imminent collapse in the demand for the work of human beings are overblown". Instead, the problem will occur in the long run, by which he means "decades, not centuries".

Cynics may feel that it is wise to make a forecast that involves some far-off but indeterminate date; it is hard for the prognosticator to be proved wrong.

The most plausible way for technological unemployment to occur is to imagine the world envisaged by Karl Marx. Wealth gets concentrated in fewer and fewer hands and this elite chooses to save, rather than spend, its income. There is a massive shortfall in demand, as there was during the era of the Great Depression, and this leads to huge job losses. But will this happen? In the past, people with great wealth surrounded themselves with staff, as viewers of any costume drama will know. Rich celebrities today tend to have an entourage, including security guards, chauffeurs, fitness trainers, chefs, hair stylists and the rest.

Admittedly, this may not be a very appealing world, in which large numbers of people are reduced to the role of domestic staff. Still, this "*Downton Abbey* with laptops" scenario seems unlikely. It is not inevitable that automation will widen inequality. It is a widely cited rule of robotics that "hard things are easy and simple things are hard". Robots can perform complex manufacturing tasks and computers can make intricate calculations, but they struggle to fold a towel or recognise a cat. That means tasks involving manual dexterity or nuanced judgment will still be reserved for people; the same is true for caring for children and the elderly. In future, the jobs that may well disappear fastest are in the professions; routine financial analysis or legal research, for example.

In his book *The AI Economy*, Roger Bootle argues that "many of the developments in the AI revolution will be pushing in the direction of reduced inequality as they undermine middle-class incomes by providing services at lower prices, thereby benefitting people lower down the income scale."[11]

The technopessimist view implicitly assumes that democratically elected governments will not reduce inequalities by higher rates of taxation, or by breaking up corporate monopolies, or that they will not create jobs for their voters. (To be fair to Mr Susskind, he does suggest that governments will need to take such actions.) But democracies tend to react to periods of high unemployment and produce new policies, rather as Franklin Roosevelt did in the 1930s. It should be possible to create jobs, whether it is insulating homes to reduce carbon emissions, caring for the elderly population, or providing more support to those with disabilities.

Optimistic commentators often cite the example of bank tellers. When Bartleby started work in 1980, part of the weekly routine was the need to queue at the bank on Thursday or Friday to get cash for the weekend. This involved writing a cheque, which would be cashed by a branch employee. When automated teller machines (ATMs) were introduced, people could get their cash much more quickly. That could have led to a huge loss of employment in bank branches. In fact, the number of jobs went up in the first couple of decades after ATMs were introduced. Banks found that ATMs made branches cheaper to operate so they opened more of them, and bank employees spent more of their time offering advice, or selling other services, to the customers.

In recent times, however, this example has become increasingly out of date. Bank branches are now closing at a rapid rate, as people rely more on online banking, with a record 3,324 US outlets closing in 2020.[12]

The broader case for optimism is that history suggests economies tend to keep creating jobs, even as the population grows and technology makes us more efficient. In 1977, around 65% of the US population, aged 15 to 64, was in work. By 2000, that proportion had grown to 74.5%, despite all the innovation in the intervening decades. The proportion then dropped but in June 2021, in the wake of the pandemic, it was still 68.9%, higher than in 1977.[13]

These figures rebut a commonly cited argument known as the "lump of labour fallacy". This states that there is only a certain amount of work to go round so that one person's job gain is another's loss. It has been used in the past to argue that women should not join the workforce (so that the jobs can be saved for the men), that immigration should be strictly controlled or even that the elderly should retire early, to create jobs for the young. But the argument misses a key point; when you pay a worker a wage, he or she spends the money and becomes a source of demand for another worker. In other words, the amount of work is not limited; it expands as our population and income grow. That is why there are plenty of jobs even though the US population has grown more than fourfold since 1900. And it also means there is no reason, in principle, why job creation cannot continue.

Training wheels

Where the pessimists are likely to be right is that existing jobs will be disrupted. A report by McKinsey estimated that 375m workers round the world would have to find new jobs because of automation.[14] Less pessimistically, the World Economic Forum, a think-tank best known for its annual summit in Davos, thinks that 85m jobs will be lost to automation by 2025, but in the process 97m new jobs will be created.[15] Job losses will be seen in areas such as data entry, accounting and administrative support but new jobs will be created in the caring professions (nurses, home help for the elderly) and in the green economy (solar engineers, wind technicians etc). Of course, the process can be deeply unpleasant for individual workers when they lose their jobs as the economy changes. A Bank of America report estimates that 100m workers may need to switch jobs by 2030.[16]

Bank of America estimates that 65% of children starting school today will work in jobs that have yet to be invented (algorithm insurer and 3D food printer chef are two of the bank's suggestions). But this will require a lot of retraining and governments are not doing enough: Denmark spends over 2% of GDP on retraining workers but the US spends only 0.1%.

The need for training means that individuals will have to be flexible to survive in the new world of work. It is tempting, when one reaches a certain age, to be "old fogeyish" when it comes to new technology. It is also foolish. Most of the new apps are designed to be used in the mass market, and thus are rarely that complicated. If you have got the hang of swiping, then you can usually manage them, and the internet is full of handy guides for the uninitiated. More generally, people need to realise the need for training throughout their careers, not just at the start.

People also need to be flexible about the sectors they are

willing to work in. There was a British TV comedy show in the 1970s called *The Wheeltappers and Shunters Social Club*, but anyone today hoping to get a job in the art of tapping a train's wheels to test their soundness would be out of luck. The McKinsey report suggests that jobs in healthcare may grow significantly by 2030 while those in production and warehousing will decline. That could be a challenge for men, who tend not to apply for jobs in some areas of the healthcare sector.

Another trend from history lends support to the optimists. As late as 1800 around 60% of the French population worked in agriculture; now it is around 2.4%.[17] As in many other countries, French agriculture has been mechanised, with tractors and combine harvesters replacing people (and horses). But the French have plenty of food to eat and the loss of farm work has not led to mass unemployment. A similar pattern happened in manufacturing. In the US, manufacturing's share of total employment in 1910 was 32.4%; by 2015, it was just 8.7%.[18] Services jobs now dominate the economy. The broad category named "other professional services" employed 3% of the workforce in 1910 but 29% by 2015.

Indeed, automation has been advancing for decades. General Motors installed a robot in a factory in 1961 and there was rapid expansion of robotics in the 1970s and 1980s. Manufacturing employment duly declined. But services jobs have replaced them. The proportion of British and Japanese in work was higher than at any time in the previous 50 years.[19]

And it is easy to forget the other advantages of automation. In the long run, the ability of some industries to produce more goods with fewer people leads to lower prices for consumers. Those consumers can then spend some of the saved money on other goods and services, providing jobs for the displaced workers. And it is not just that goods are cheaper; consumers can purchase new products. Before the automation of the textile industry in the early 19th century, cotton clothes were so expensive that they were the preserve of the rich.

Demography too is on the side of the workers (and the optimists). The birth rate has been dropping for decades and took a further downward plunge during the pandemic. That means there are fewer new workers joining the workforce, while the baby boomers (those born between 1945 and 1964) are retiring. The effect of this shift was overshadowed in the 1990s and 2000s by the entry of China, with its hundreds of millions of workers, into the global market. But China is ageing too. Over the next 30 years the working-age population will fall, as a proportion of the total, by three percentage points in the US, five points in Britain, seven in the EU and in Japan, and 11 in China.[20]

In the short term, the pandemic gave workers bargaining power. This was slightly surprising given that many feared that covid would lead to mass unemployment. But the swift action taken by governments to protect workers' incomes during the crisis indicated that politicians realised they needed to favour labour a bit more and business a bit less if they wanted to stay in office. Even parties on the right have been willing to sound aggressive towards the business sector. Donald Trump displayed immense dislike towards some of the big tech companies and Boris Johnson proclaimed "Fuck business" when told about corporate concerns over the risks of Brexit.

Furlough schemes maintained workers' incomes during the crisis. Even though the schemes did not offer 100% income replacement, the lockdowns meant that people's spending fell at least as much as their income, as they had less need to travel and could not spend money in restaurants or bars. When the first lockdown ended, many workers decided not to return to jobs in hospitality or construction, from which they had been laid off, and this led to a bidding war for labour in some sectors. In the spring of 2021, salaries at British hospitality and catering firms were up 18% on the previous year. In the US, job vacancies were at their highest levels in two decades, even though unemployment was above its pre-pandemic levels. Data from the New York Fed showed that the reservation wage (the minimum amount people needed to be tempted into the labour market) had jumped $10,000 in the year to March 2021 (although it fell back later in the year).[21] Some of this may be temporary and linked to the greater generosity of benefits during the crisis. But the trend may also be caused by a preference for flexible jobs and a realisation that there are other options than low-paid insecure work.

The pandemic did lead to lost jobs, but not as many as might have been feared given the immediate hit to GDP. Nor did automation surge as rapidly as might have been expected. Rockwell Automation, a world leader in industrial robots, suffered a sales decline of 5.5% in 2020; an analysis by *The Economist* in early 2021 found that there were 900,000 extra routine jobs in the US than might have been expected had the previous trend continued.[22]

To take a longer-term perspective, mass unemployment

occurs when the economy takes a downturn, usually because consumer demand has been hit. This means that there is less demand for goods and services, and employers lay off workers. In turn, these layoffs reduce demand. Governments aim to break the cycle by increasing public spending or cutting taxes to put money in consumers' pockets (fiscal policy); broadly speaking, the approach favoured by the economist John Maynard Keynes. On top of that, central banks will reduce interest rates to persuade consumers and businesses to save less and borrow more (monetary policy). Eventually, demand picks up and unemployment falls. For prolonged technological unemployment to occur, this would suggest that fiscal and monetary policy no longer work.

The personal touch

Another hopeful possibility is that automation may lead to a reaction among consumers. They may tire of mass-produced goods and prefer those that display the human touch. The clash between crafts and mechanisation has been noticeable since the early days of the Industrial Revolution. At first, it looked as if mechanisation was bound to triumph. At the Great Exhibition in 1851, British producers were startled by the quality of goods from the US, which used the "American system" of machine-tooled parts. The predictable quality of such components was very useful for arms manufacturers.

In the late 19th century, there was a reaction to automation in the form of the arts and crafts movement, led by William Morris. Something similar happened in the 1970s and may be happening again. Think of all the shops that sell "artisan" loaves or cheese, the bars that sell beer from microbreweries or, at the top end of the market, the enthusiasm for designer clothes. These are niche markets, admittedly. But there is another section of the market that likes to buy locally, or in an environmentally sustainable fashion, which may favour craftspeople of the type that appear on the British television show *The Repair Shop* where family heirlooms are lovingly restored to life.

It is also significant that craft-type jobs tend to be more satisfying for workers because they require more creativity and give individuals more control over the process. These were qualities possessed by some trades (blacksmiths, carpenters, tailors) well before the Industrial Revolution. Automation can also help by reducing the more tedious aspects of some careers, and thus make the rest of the job feel more rewarding. And it also replaces some jobs that were pure drudgery; operating the till at a supermarket, or working as a secretary in a typing pool, were not particularly fulfilling tasks, for example. But a new category of jobs has emerged, where workers operate in a kind of limbo, neither free agents nor full-time employees. That is the issue we turn to next.

THE FUTURE OF
WORK. PART 2

Working conditions are not just a matter for employers and employees. The pandemic prompted unprecedented intervention by some governments in the labour market. In some cases, through the operation of "furlough schemes", they subsidised the wages of workers in the private sector to prevent a sudden jump in unemployment. That raises a broader question. Will governments intervene in the labour market more often in normal times, to push for higher wages and better working conditions?

There is a long-running debate within the field of economics about the impact of government regulations on employment. Those in the purist, free-market camp argue that jobs represent a contract between company and employee, freely entered into on both sides. If a job is too onerous, or pays too little, the company will fail to attract workers. Similarly, if companies discriminate against women, or against people from other ethnic groups or of different religions, they will be at a competitive disadvantage versus rivals that can choose employees from a much wider (and more talented) pool. The market will sort everything out.

By contrast, the purists argue, if the government intervenes to protect workers by installing laws limiting hours, or a minimum wage, the effect will be to dissuade companies from hiring workers at all. Instead, they will automate as much as possible to keep their costs down.

On the left, the argument is that companies and workers do not negotiate as equals. Job-seekers cannot afford to wait a few months to assess the best opportunities; they have rent to pay and families to feed today and tomorrow. If they complain about the job and quit, or get fired, that may constitute a black mark on their record and prevent them from being hired elsewhere. There is also an asymmetry of information. Companies may be using dangerous machinery or chemicals, with effects that become clear to workers only much later. When workers attempt to band together in unions to negotiate from strength, companies often resist. Look back over history, and governments have been forced to intervene to protect workers by stopping child labour, imposing limits on working hours or legislating for equal pay for women.

It is clear that an extreme "free market" position has little public support and has not been borne out by events. Take, for example, the idea that a minimum wage would lead to a sharp decline in employment. In 1992, 79% of US economists thought this was the case.[1] Since then, however, studies have found the relationship is far from clear; when New Jersey raised its minimum wage, but neighbouring Pennsylvania did not, employment in the former state's fast food restaurants went up, not down. In the average rich country, the minimum wage has climbed from 35% of average earnings in

2000 to 41% in 2019 without triggering the tsunami of job losses that might have been anticipated.[2]

This development might seem to break the laws of supply and demand. But in some cases, employers may have such bargaining power that they can hold workers' wages below the "right" level; in other words, they pay workers less than they contribute to the business and not enough to attract unemployed people to apply for jobs. When authorities impose a minimum wage, companies can still be profitable and more people may be drawn into the labour market by the chance to earn more.[3] In some cases, a higher wage may reduce staff turnover and encourage greater productivity (as workers put in more effort if they feel they are being fairly rewarded).[4]

But it would be foolish to believe that government interventions have no adverse impact on job creation. The continental European model tends to have strong workers' rights, making it very difficult for employers to lay people off, and requiring them to offer sick pay and several weeks' holiday. In addition, companies have to contribute, on the workers' behalf, to government benefit schemes. This latter figure, the "tax wedge", is around a third of the cost of employing a worker in the rich world.[5] The additional costs, and the difficulty in firing an unproductive employee, may deter companies from taking on new workers in the first place. The result seems to be an insider–outsider employment market, with good conditions for those in work but a large pool of unemployed. The US model gives workers fewer rights but means it is easier to find some sort of a job.

In the fancy euphemisms used by economists, cutting

workers' rights is known as enhancing "labour market flex-ibility". An International Monetary Fund study, which studied 97 countries over the 1980–2008 period, found that "policies aimed at increasing labour market flexibility may have an important effect in reducing unemployment".[6]

Some jobs are clearly better than no jobs but the worry is that many people are stuck in low-paid, unfulfilling and insecure jobs, a class dubbed the "precariat". US gig economy workers were twice as likely as other employees to be in low-paid jobs and were two-thirds less likely to have a retirement plan.[7]

That, of course, explains why the gig economy has devel-oped in the first place; companies find it cheaper. They can employ workers as freelance contractors, without having to offer holiday pay, health benefits and the rest. By paying their workers less, such firms can undercut companies that offer their employees greater protection. Again, this can give socie-ties a difficult choice. Should they ban such work and take the risk of lower overall employment? The courts have started to rule that some groups, such as Uber drivers, are entitled to more rights because they are effectively working for a single company.

These issues are bound to recur over the coming decades. One of the most striking features of the internet has been the ability to link customers with service providers through platforms. These platforms remove a lot of the hassle and, in theory, make it far easier for both parties. In the days before Uber, someone needing a cab would have a limited number of choices. They could try to hail one on the street, but that only worked if they were in a city centre and was often impossible in peak hours or when it was raining. Or they could search the phone book for a minicab service and hope that they had a car available ("Be with you in 25 minutes, mate," always seemed to be the answer). Uber was much more convenient. Given that Uber rides tend to be much cheaper than traditional taxis, the result has been a much-expanded market for ride-hailing.

Similarly, the internet made it easier to find plumbers, decorators, electricians etc. and to see how other customers have rated their work. In turn, this may have reduced the need for workers, and firms, to advertise or market their services. People with spare time can find work to do through platforms such as TaskRabbit, and those with creative skills can find customers on platforms like Etsy. In aggregate, this increased the productivity of the economy by enabling people to make money in their spare time.

The appeal of companies

In a classic paper, "The nature of the firm", written in 1937, Ronald Coase posed the question of why so much economic activity was organised within companies.[8] After all, much economic theory revolves around the idea of incentives: for example, workers move from one company to another in pursuit of higher wages. But that doesn't happen within a firm. Many people move from one activity to another, without the incentive of higher pay, because the management tells them to do so. And managers do not turn to the markets to hire new employees for each task even if, in theory, they might get more skilful workers by doing so.

Coase's explanation for this phenomenon was that

markets may be suitable for standardised activities, but not for less well-defined ones. To negotiate separate contracts for each activity would be time-consuming and messy. It is cheaper and more efficient to hire workers on longer-term contracts and then direct their activities, he argued.[9] But the advent of the internet, and indeed the mobile phone, has reduced the costs and the hassle of relying on the markets to hire workers for short-time tasks as the gig economy demonstrates. As a result, the proportion of workers who are self-employed, or are on short-term contracts, may be set to rise inexorably.

There are significant potential drawbacks to this shift. By drawing more labour into the market, the gig economy has reduced the bargaining power, and thus the wages, of existing workers. Before the pandemic, the balance of power seemed to have shifted in favour of employers and customers. In Britain, surveys by the Living Wage Foundation discovered that 37% of workers were given less than a week's notice of their shifts or work patterns.[10] About 7% of all workers had less than 24 hours' notice. That would be a struggle for anyone who has to care for children or elderly relatives. Couple that with the low pay associated with these jobs and many consumers and investors feel uneasy about these companies; when Deliveroo, the food delivery group, floated on the London stock market in early 2021, many institutional investors turned down the chance to buy the shares.

It is hard to believe, however, that the gig economy will disappear. Enough consumers like the convenience and low prices it brings to offset those who might have scruples about the conditions endured by workers. And it is also the case that the gig economy provides a chance for many people to get a foothold in the labour market. A 2018 study of London Uber drivers found that the vast majority were male immigrants, drawn from the lower half of the income distribution.[11] They earned around £11 an hour and half of them said their incomes had increased by working for Uber; on average they reported higher levels of life satisfaction than other workers.

Some feel that few modern jobs are fulfilling. That was the view taken by the late anthropologist David Graeber, in his 2018 book *Bullshit Jobs*.[12] Mr Graeber argued that many of us were stuck in meaningless work, which made us bored and depressed. Based on a couple of surveys, he found that up to 40% of us believed our jobs "did not make a meaningful contribution to the world" and that, if you add it in the pointless parts of other people's work (responding to e-mails etc.), more than half of our collective effort may be bullshit. This pointless effort was the result of "managerial feudalism" whereby executives hired lots of lackeys to maintain their prestige (a clear echo of C. Northcote Parkinson) while young graduates were forced into such meaningless work to pay off their student debt.

Although much of this book has bemoaned the tedium of office life, Bartleby still feels that Mr Graeber's thesis was overstated. Yes, most jobs have their frustrating aspects but that is not to say they are completely pointless. And the sectors that Mr Graeber dismissed as bullshit were the ones that one might expect a leftish academic to dislike – finance and marketing, for example. Plenty of people in finance might retort that they pay a lot of taxes, and export a lot of services, so that the state can afford to pay for academics in "bullshit" subjects like anthropology. (Job snobbery is a long-established trait. Aristocrats tended to look down on those people who were "in trade"; Napoleon dismissed Britain as "a nation of shopkeepers"; bureaucrats are dismissed as "pen-pushers" and accountants as "bean-counters"; skilled workers looked down on the unskilled; and business executives are dismissive of those who work in the public sector.)

Three academics who looked into Mr Graeber's thesis found there was very little evidence in its favour.[13] When they analysed the European Working Conditions Survey, which interviewed 44,000 workers in 28 countries in 2015, they found that only 4.4% answered "rarely" or "never" to the question "Do you think your work is useful?" Rather than rising over time, as Mr Graeber suggested, this proportion had fallen from 7.8% in 2005. Furthermore, this feeling of uselessness was most prevalent, not in the sectors Mr Graeber suggested, but in low-paid roles like cleaning which he had argued were socially beneficial. As to the role of student debt, the academics found that British graduates (who are particularly indebted) were only half as likely as non-graduates to feel useless.

There is a lot going on here. The "managerial feudalism" thesis seems inherently implausible as executives tend to be motivated by share options, which in turn depend on rising profits. So executives have every interest in keeping down employment costs and are hardly likely to recruit lots of useless people. Indeed, the more normal criticism of late 20th and early 21st century capitalism is that managers have been obsessed with cutting jobs.

Meaningless jobs are more likely to occur where there

is no competition, which is not really a private-sector trait. Think back to the communist countries of eastern Europe where workers joked: "We pretend to work and they pretend to pay us." The Japanese corporate sector long had a "jobs for life" culture in which salarymen were paid just to sit in the office. But its multinationals focused on expanding sales rather than maximising profits. When he formed his laws, Northcote Parkinson focused his attention on government bureaucracies that had every incentive to multiply their staff and seemingly little constraint on their ability to do so. Meaningless jobs also occur in absolute monarchies or among the staff of the very rich, who have lots of hangers-on. But these weren't the jobs that Mr Graeber was targeting.

Furthermore, the survey question which Mr Graeber relied on ("Does your job make a meaningful contribution to the world?") seems a very high bar to clear. Many people would be too modest to claim such a thing. But they are still likely to feel that their job is useful, if only to their colleagues.

The academics who analysed Graeber's work argue that the real problem is not "bullshit jobs" but the Marxist idea of "alienation". The concept dates back to when artisans ceased to use their own tools to work for themselves and flocked to factories to use machines owned by the capitalist class. In the modern sense, workers tend to feel alienated, and thus useless, if they believe that their efforts are not appreciated, that managers do not listen to them, and if they have little autonomy about how they perform their tasks. In other words, a feeling of alienation is much more about bad management than about workers' perceptions about the perceived social usefulness of their roles. This brings us back to a theme of the book: work is much more enjoyable if employees feel their efforts are appreciated.

A lack of respect and autonomy is much more likely to beset workers in low-skilled jobs than for the graduates to whom Mr Graeber was referring. Many of those graduates eventually come to believe in their usefulness to society, even if they are investment bankers or management consultants, two roles that Mr Graeber felt were overpaid and parasitical. Work in any business long enough and you are likely to absorb its culture. If you don't, you will probably leave.

So the outlook for the employment market in future decades will result from the interplay of two forces: the demographic shift leading to fewer workers (with more bargaining power) and the structural shift towards shorter-term contracts (giving them less).

The future is remote?

As already noted, the covid-19 pandemic caused an immense and immediate change in working habits. People in office jobs were required by governments to work from home. Previously anybody who opted to work from home, on more than the occasional day, was likely to be viewed with suspicion. But now managers were doing it as well as their teams. And they found ways of making it work. This was hardly surprising. Documents could be shared instantly (and edited simultaneously); meetings could still be held. The technology to do so had been around for years. It was just the willingness that was lacking. A survey by investment bank Morgan Stanley found that across five European countries (Britain, France, Germany, Italy and Spain), 62% of office employees were working from home, on at least one day a week, in the spring of 2021.[14] That compared with 32% before the pandemic.

To the surprise of many observers, productivity did not appear to decline, at least according to surveys. In early 2021, the Chartered Institute of Personnel and Development found that 33% of employers thought that remote working had boosted productivity, compared with 23% who thought it had declined.[15] But this survey-based response is open to question. Workers may have produced as much output as before, but they seem to have taken more hours to do so. Under the standard economic definition, productivity (as measured by output per hour) may really have dropped.

Academics who monitored 10,000 professionals at an Asian technology company found that they worked 30% more hours to produce the same output.[16] Part of the problem was that they spent a lot more time in meetings which cut into the time they could use for productive work. This survey involved software that monitored what employees were actually doing, which enhances its credibility; however, the work involved was quite technical and may have suffered more than most from the loss of face-to-face collaboration. Perhaps if the managers of this company had not called so many meetings, productivity might not have suffered.

More generally, many employees found they enjoyed the experience of working from home. In Britain, the Reed employment agency found that in 2021 people were twice as likely to apply for a job vacancy if it was advertised as remote.[17] Of course, it is possible that the pandemic may prove a blip and everything returns to normal, but it is clear that most workers would prefer that didn't happen. Surveys suggest US workers would like to spend half the week at home.[18]

Potentially a shift to remote working is an enormously positive development. For 200 years since we started to file into factories, humans have slaved under the tyranny of the clock. Before 1800, we were paid for what we produced: grain, vegetables, shoes, textiles and so on. But in the modern era, we are paid for our time. Our time is literally no longer our own. The company determines the hours when we work and that in turn affects the time when we wake in the morning, eat our meals and see our families and friends.

The tyranny of the clock has also meant that most people travel to and from work at roughly the same time. Working from home saves employees from the daily commute, whether wedged into a packed train or sitting and fuming in a traffic jam. A survey that asked people to evaluate their time use found that the morning and evening commute were two of the least pleasurable activities (the other one was working itself).[19] To the extent that people commute in cars (around 86% of Americans do so), home working is also better for the environment.[20]

Home working means that people can pick up their kids from school, can be around when parcels are delivered and repairmen arrive, and, for those who have a garden, they can sit in the sunshine. Those who tend to wake early can get some work done before breakfast; night owls can take a break in the day and work when everybody else has gone to bed. In theory, this is a huge advance for human freedom.

For employers, home working means they can save on

office space, a significant cost; if people are coming in only three days a week, the space needed falls in theory by 40%. And the evidence suggests that offices were not being fully used even before the pandemic; Cushman & Wakefield, a property consultant, estimated that global office occupancy was only around 60%. In particular, the top executives were often flying round the world to visit subsidiaries or meet clients, leaving a lot of pricey space unoccupied.

The cost reductions could be even greater in the long run. Many industries tend to cluster in certain places: finance in London and New York and technology in the area around San Francisco. As high-skilled workers move to these districts, property prices are pushed higher, along with the cost of many other services. In turn, this drives up wages for workers in other sectors, as companies need to pay them enough to meet the higher cost of living. But if people can work from home, there is no need for companies to pay this wage premium; they can recruit workers who live in rural Devon or Kentucky and who will be happy to accept a lower salary. In August 2021, Google developed a pay calculator to tell employees how much less they would earn if they worked from home or moved offices to a less expensive location; one employee who faced a two-hour commute to the Seattle office found that his pay would be cut by 10% if he worked at home.[21]

The shift could be bad for some existing employees but could benefit others if jobs are created outside the big cities, "levelling up" the economies of some developed nations. Poor people who cannot afford big-city rents might benefit. A study by McKinsey found that 70% of companies thought that remote working would allow them to increase the diversity of their staff.[22] At the height of the pandemic, there was talk of an "exodus" from cities, although the cultural aspects of urban living (entertainment venues, restaurants, bars) will still appeal to many. Of course, there is also the possibility that companies could recruit workers for even lower wages in Asia and Africa; this has already happened with some back-office administrative roles, on top of the better-known example of call centres.

But some things are undoubtedly missing when people work at home. Individuals start to feel isolated from the rest of the team and companies struggle to create any sense of team spirit. It may well be (although this is hard to prove) that creativity occurs when people from different departments meet in the corridors or at the coffee machine; such spontaneity will not occur when everyone is at home. Nor, indeed, will office romances.

Not everyone can take advantage of the flexibility of remote working in the same way. It suits well-paid professionals who own houses big enough to allow them to work in a separate room from other people, and who can afford a good broadband package. In effect, companies are passing on to employees the cost of heat, power and light during the working day. Younger people who share a flat may find it more difficult to find space and thus to concentrate. Parents may also find it difficult to combine home working with childcare; even if they employ someone to look after their kids, children will be tempted to interrupt their parents if they know they are only a few feet away. A survey by Gartner of British employees found that 42% of those who worked remotely felt emotionally drained as a result. This has led to some companies adopting policies such as "no-meeting half days" to try to relieve the pressure.

But it is clear that the conventional working day will not return for many people. Instead, the future may consist of "hybrid working" with employees travelling to the office on three or four days a week and spending the other one or two days at home. A survey by Envoy and Wakefield Research of 1,000 workers in the UK in the spring of 2021 found that 34% thought that hybrid working would improve their mental health while 41% thought it would improve their work–life balance. Just over half (55%) of respondents said they would look for another job if their employer did not offer a hybrid approach with the proportion rising to 78% among younger workers.[23] Separate research by Barclays, based on 4,300 office workers in six countries, found that the desire to have a hybrid working pattern was uniform across sectors, countries and genders. The evidence suggests companies will let them. The Chartered Institute of Personnel and Development found that 63% of employers planned to continue the use of hybrid working even after the pandemic.[24]

This will allow plenty of scope for the collaboration needed for teams to work, while reducing commute times, giving employees some flexibility and allowing them time to concentrate on particular projects without being disturbed by the office buzz. Video conferencing means they will still be able to join in meetings, alongside those who are already in the office.

Clearly some co-ordination will be needed. If hybrid working means less office space, there won't be room for everyone to attend on the same day; people will have to reserve their desks. There will be a great temptation for many people to opt for Fridays or Mondays as one of their working from home days, to make it a long weekend, which means that Wednesdays may be the crunch points for office space. The savings for companies may be limited by the need to redesign office space to include more meeting rooms, "break-out areas" (for small teams) and pods (for solitary working); these will help lure workers into the office.

The change in working patterns is not just about days; it is also about hours. According to Bank of America, nearly all the 10m jobs created in the US between 2005 and 2015 were outside the traditional 9-to-5 format. This shift creates its own momentum. If some businesses are able to offer services 24 hours a day, seven days a week, they will gain market share from companies with more restricted hours. So there will be pressure to follow the trend. In turn these shift workers will have to adjust the hours when they consume goods and services, creating new demand for all-day services.

It is also worth noting that lots of employees are unable to work at home. If you drive a delivery van, work in a hospital or on a factory floor, you have to be physically present at work. So there is an obvious danger of a two-tier market divided between those employees who enjoy the benefits of flexibility and those who have flexibility imposed upon them. Such contracts create a pool of labour that employers can call on if needed; something similar used to apply at ports, with foremen selecting from a crowd of dockers at the gate every morning. This is extremely flexible for the employer but gives no guarantee of income for the worker. For some people, this flexibility may be OK as they are only seeking a small amount of work; they can turn down a shift, if offered. But if you depend on your job to pay your food and rent every month, you are likely to take anything on offer, even if the hours are inconvenient, the conditions unsafe and the income poor.

In summary, the future of work will depend on which country and which sector you work in. The more skills you have, the more in demand you will be, and the greater the likelihood that companies will offer you the kind of flexibility you desire. But those conditions may apply to only a minority of the workforce. A much bigger group will find themselves at the mercy of low pay and irregular hours, working in sectors that are subject to cut-throat price competition. However, those who provide personal face-to-face services are much less likely to find their jobs automated than those who analyse data or shuffle paperwork.

Wherever you work, the chances are that some of the irritations mentioned in this book – endless meetings, pointless jargon, meandering training sessions – will still plague you. But there is hope. Even if they don't read this book, managers may steadily learn that wasting the time of their employees doesn't achieve anything for them or their company. Treating people with kindness and intelligence makes sense.

BARTLEBY'S RULES

This book has both reviewed the irritations of working life and proposed a number of rules that describe them. It is worth repeating and reviewing them here.

Bartleby's law. This asserts that 80% of the time spent by 80% of people in meetings is wasted. Too many meetings are called, involving too many people, and they last too long. The implication of this law is that both productivity and morale will improve if meetings are fewer and shorter. The same principle applies to training schemes devoted to non-technical issues; managers should think twice before making employees sit through them.

An update to Parkinson's law as applied to remote working. The original Parkinson's law is that work expands to fill the time available. In part, this is because workers in an office know they are under the boss's eye. Remote working removes this problem and creates two responses, depending on whether the worker is a slacker or a Stakhanovite. When it comes to slackers: "For the unconcerned, when unobserved, work shrinks to fill the time required." But when it comes to Stakhanovites: "Work expands to fill all their waking hours." In addition, for bosses: "Zoom expands to fill all of the manager's available time."

The Bartleby curse. This is an update to the Peter principle which states that people get promoted to their level of incompetence. The curse is a cautionary tale for those who pursue promotion so vigorously that their working days become consumed with meetings and they cease to do the kind of work that satisfies them. In short: "People get promoted until they reach a level when they stop enjoying their jobs."

The law of corporate gobbledegook. "Jargon abhors a vacuum." When executives and managers have nothing substantial to say, they use obscure words and obfuscatory language to fill the space.

Bartleby's rule on advisers. There are lots of people who offer advice to companies ranging from investment bankers to management consultants. These advisers charge high fees but it is far from clear whether companies really benefit, and workers often lose out. Hence the rule that such advice is nearly always a better deal for the advisers than for the advised.

If there are two underlying principles behind these rules, they are: "Don't waste people's time" and "Don't be an asshole." If managers could absorb these lessons, our working lives would be a lot more pleasant. We could spend less time in meetings, whether in person or on video, and get on with our actual tasks. We would spend less time and energy trying to climb the corporate ladder and focus more on the work that we find enjoyable. And we would speak clearly and not hide our meaning behind vacuous terminology.

It is a tough quest, since the pressures are nearly always in the opposite direction, as this book has tried to explain. Perhaps because the nature of modern office work is hard to define, it is easy to fill our time with meetings, or to focus on time spent, rather than goals achieved. And because many jobs are not related to the production of physical goods, it is tempting to use jargon to make our efforts sound more important.

But what this book has also tried to demonstrate is that these practices make companies less efficient, not more so. Meetings waste time and tire people mentally, so making gatherings less frequent and shorter will make workers more productive. Promoting people to positions where they will be unhappy doesn't make sense either. And the use of jargon just means workers are unable to understand what the company is trying to do.

These customs can change precisely because they are not essential to the conduct of office work. A few meetings may be necessary and some technical language is required; it may be impossible to predict which people will make good managers in advance. But plenty of companies get by with a minimum of meetings and with a more laissez-faire approach to office attendance, recognising that what really matters is whether people get the work done on time. The pandemic showed that many employees could work remotely.

Another important message is that the "macho" style of

management is no longer effective, if it ever was. The modern manager is a coach, bringing out the best in the team. The role model is Gareth Southgate, the England football manager, rather than Donald Trump or Jack Welch. This model still requires some hard decisions; if people do not perform to the required standard, they will have to be moved or even fired. But it does involve explanation and empathy, rather than shouting and domination. The manager should have a strong enough personality to make business judgments but not so much of an ego as to believe they are solely responsible for the team's success.

Of course, some of the corporate talk about diversity and sustainability will be waffle. Companies should be judged by their actions, rather than their words. Even then, it is a lot easier for some companies (a software firm, for example) to have a "zero carbon footprint" than for a steel producer. Or take the example of inequality, as measured by the ratio between executive and worker pay; a company that subcontracts its cleaning and security services so those staff don't appear on its payroll can look a lot more egalitarian than one that doesn't.

But it is still encouraging that companies are trying to think more about these issues. They are thinking about the diversity of their staff, the work–life balance of their employees, their impact on the environment and so on. All this means it could not just become more pleasant to work in the corporate sector but employees could feel better about the tasks they are undertaking.

For all the mockery in this book, the author recognises that we need companies, managers and indeed bureaucrats.

But it would be better for us all if they thought more clearly about what they are doing. One can only hope that they don't decide to consider these issues in a series of long Zoom meetings.

NOTES

Introduction

1   *Simple Sabotage Field Manual* (US Office of Strategic Services) 1944, www.openculture.com/2015/12/simple-sabotage-field-manual. html

1 Getting started

1   "Olivia Bland's web applications UK interview 'humiliating'", BBC News, January 31st 2019, www.bbc.co.uk/news/ uk-england-manchester-47071423

2   "50 most common interview questions & how to answer", Glassdoor, August 31st 2021, www.glassdoor. co.uk/blog/50-common-interview-questions/?utm_ source=newsletter&utm_medium=email&utm_content=0526_ interview_prep_uk_2&utm_campaign=may21_uk

3   Frank Schmidt and John Hunter, "The validity and utility of selection methods in personnel psychology: practical and theoretical implications of 85 years of research findings", *Psychological Bulletin* 124(2) 1998

4   Greg Lewis, "5 new interviewing techniques that you should start using", LinkedIn, January 29th 2018, www. linkedin.com/business/talent/blog/talent-acquisition/ new-interviewing-techniques-that-you-need-to-know-about

5   Kate Rockwood, "Assessing personalities", SHRM, February 29th 2020, www.shrm.org/hr-today/news/all-things-work/pages/personality-assessments.aspx

6   Adam Bryant, "Walt Bettinger of Charles Schwab: you've got to open up to move up", *Wall Street Journal*, February 4th 2016

7   Madhumita Murgia, "Emotion recognition: can AI detect human feelings from a face?", *Financial Times*, May 12th 2021

8   Karen Hao, "Facebook's ad-serving algorithm discriminates by gender and race", *MIT Technology Review*, April 5th 2019

9   Caroline Criado Perez, *Invisible Women: Exposing Data Bias in a World Designed for Men* (Chatto & Windus) 2019

10   Jennifer Eberhardt, *Biased: The New Science of Race and Inequality* (Penguin) 2020

11   Dina Gerdeman, "Minorities who 'whiten' job resumés get more interviews", *Harvard Business School*, May 17th 2017

12   Stefanie Johnson, David Hekman and Elsa Chan, "If there's only one woman in your candidate pool, there's statistically no chance she'll be hired", *Harvard Business Review*, April 26th 2016, hbr.org/2016/04/if-theres-only-one-woman-in-your-candidate-pool-theres-statistically-no-chance-shell-be-hired

13   "Hair-straightening products contain potentially harmful chemicals", *Harvard T. H. Chan School of Public Health*, 2018, www.hsph.harvard.edu/news/hsph-in-the-news/hair-straightening-products-chemicals/

14   Christy Zhou Koval and Ashleigh Shelby Rosette, "The natural hair bias in recruitment", *Social Psychological and Personality Science*, August 19th 2020

15   Paul Ziobro, "UPS lifts ban on beards in diversity push", *Wall Street Journal*, November 10th 2020

16   Shelley Correll, Stephen Benard and In Palk, "Getting a job: is there a motherhood penalty?", *American Journal of Sociology* 112(5) 2007

17   Joann Lublin, *Power Moms: How Executive Mothers Navigate Work and Life* (Harper Business) 2021

18 Criado Perez, *Invisible Women*, op. cit.

19 Rachel Gillett, "Sexual harassment isn't a Hollywood, tech, or media issue – it affects everyone", *Business Insider*, November 30th 2017

20 Maya Oppenheim, "Half of women report unwanted sexual behaviour at work, damning YouGov survey finds", *Independent*, June 29th 2021

21 Stephen Martin and Joseph Marks, *Messengers: Who We Listen to, Who We Don't, and Why* (Random House Business) 2019

22 Curt Rice, "How blind auditions help orchestras to eliminate gender bias", *Guardian*, October 14th 2013

23 Edward Chang et al., "The mixed effects of online diversity training", *Proceedings of the National Academy of Sciences* 116(16) April 2019, www.pnas.org/content/116/16/7778

24 "An investor's guide to diversity", privately circulated research note, March 2021

25 Christina Underhill, "The effectiveness of mentoring programs in corporate settings: a meta-analytical review of the literature", *Journal of Vocational Behaviour*, 68(2) April 2006

26 Katrinn Bennhold, "Another Side of #MeToo: male managers fearful of mentoring women", *New York Times*, January 27th 2019

27 Prudy Gourguechon, "Why in the world would men stop mentoring women post #MeToo?", *Forbes*, August 6th 2018

2 Meetings

1   Martin Lindstrom, *The Ministry of Common Sense: How to Eliminate Bureaucratic Red Tape, Bad Excuses and Corporate Bullshit* (John Murray) 2021

2   Catherine Nixey, "Hell is other people: a monk's guide to office life", *1843 magazine*, July 14th 2021

3   *Simple Sabotage Field Manual* (US Office of Strategic Services) 1944, www.openculture.com/2015/12/simple-sabotage-field-manual. html

4   Vignesh Ramachandran, "Stanford researchers identify four

causes for 'Zoom fatigue' and their simple fixes", *Stanford News*, February 23rd 2021, news.stanford.edu/2021/02/23/four-causes-zoom-fatigue-solutions/

5   "The future of meetings", *The Economist*, September 4th 2021

6   Dan Grabham, "After a long wait, the Amazon Echo Show 10 is finally going on sale", *Pocket-lint*, January 27th 2021, www.pocket-lint.com/smart-home/news/amazon/155517-after-a-long-wait-the-amazon-echo-show-10-is-finally-going-on-sale

7   Adrian Wooldridge, "Online meetings are even duller than real ones", *1843 magazine*, May 26th 2020

8   Jason Fried and David Heinemeier Hansson, *It Doesn't Have to be Crazy at Work* (HarperCollins) 2018

9   Lindstrom, *The Ministry of Common Sense,* op. cit.

10 James Citrin and Darleen DeRosa, *Leading at a Distance: Practical Lessons for Virtual Success* (Wiley) 2021

11 Jon Baker, *Running Meetings that Make Things Happen: How to Get Your Whole Team Involved, Whether Introvert or Extrovert,* 2020

12 Lindstrom, *The Ministry of Common Sense,* op. cit.

13 Taylor Locke, "Jeff Bezos: this is the 'smartest thing we ever did' at Amazon", *Make It,* October 14th 2019, www.cnbc.com/2019/10/14/jeff-bezos-this-is-the-smartest-thing-we-ever-did-at-amazon.html

14 "What is a daily scrum?", Scrum.org, www.scrum.org/resources/what-is-a-daily-scrum

15 "Standup meetings can be a waste of time & what to do about it", Geekbot, April 29th 2020, geekbot.com/blog/standup-meetings-waste-of-time/

16 Irving Janis, *Victims of Groupthink: A Psychological Study of Foreign Policy Decisions and Fiascos* (Houghton Mifflin Harcourt) 1972

17 Gary Klein, Tim Koller and Dan Lovallo, "Bias busters. Premortems: being smart at the start", *McKinsey Quarterly*, April 3rd 2019, www.mckinsey.com/business-functions/strategy-and-corporate-finance/our-insights/bias-busters-premortems-being-smart-at-the-start

3 Office life

1   Angus Montgomery, "Inside Facebook's new HQ – 'the largest open floor plan in the world'", *Design Week*, April 8th 2015

2   Ibid.

3   Kerstin Sailer, Petros Koutsolampros and Rosica Pachilova, "Differential perceptions of teamwork, focused work and perceived productivity as an effect of desk characteristics within a workplace layout", April 28th 2021, journals.plos.org/plosone/article?id=10.1371/journal.pone.0250058

4   Ethan Bernstein and Stephen Turban, "The impact of the 'open' workspace on human collaboration", *Philosophical Transactions of the Royal Society B*, July 2nd 2018, royalsocietypublishing.org/doi/10.1098/rstb.2017.0239

5   Matthew Zeitlin, "Why WeWork went wrong", *Guardian*, December 20th 2019

6   Annie Palmer, "WeWork CEO returns $5.9 million the company paid him for 'We' trademark", CNBC, September 4th 2019, www.cnbc.com/2019/09/04/wework-ceo-returns-5point9-million-the-company-paid-for-we-trademark.html

7   George Hammond, "WeWork loses $2.1bn and sheds members as lockdowns bite", *Financial Times*, May 20th 2021

8   Robert Armstrong, "Junior Goldman Sachs bankers complain of 95-hour week", *Financial Times*, March 18th 2021

9   Emily Guendelsberger, *On the Clock: What Low-Wage Work Did to Me and How It Drives America Insane* (Little, Brown) 2019

10   Andrew Edgecliffe-Johnson, "'Amazon effect' sets the tone for US workers' remuneration", *Financial Times*, June 23rd 2021

11   Tobias Baer and Simone Schnall, "Quantifying the cost of decision fatigue: suboptimal risk decisions in finance", *Royal Society Open Science*, May 5th 2021, royalsocietypublishing.org/doi/10.1098/rsos.201059

12   Lisa Evans, "How your 'always busy' pace is ruining your decision-making", Fast Company, September

29th 2014, www.fastcompany.com/3036269/
how-your-always-busy-pace-is-ruining-your-decision-making

13 Felicity Hannah, "Unlimited holiday: a perk that comes with
pitfalls", BBC News, February 22nd 2019, www.bbc.co.uk/news/
business-47338096

14 "Study: a record 768 million U.S. vacation days went unused in '18,
opportunity cost in the billions", US Travel Association, August
16th 2019, www.ustravel.org/press/study-record-768-million-us-
vacation-days-went-unused-18-opportunity-cost-billions

15 "Work-life balance", Better Life Index, www.oecdbetterlifeindex.
org/topics/work-life-balance/

16 Health and Safety Executive, "Causes of stress at work", www.hse.
gov.uk/stress/causes.htm

17 Health and Safety Executive, "Health priority plan: work-related
stress", www.hse.gov.uk/aboutus/strategiesandplans/health-and-
work-strategy/work-related-stress.pdf

18 "42 worrying workplace stress statistics", American
Institute of Stress, September 25th 2019, www.stress.
org/42-worrying-workplace-stress-statistics

19 Blake Thorne, "How distractions at work take up more time than
you think", I Done This, February 13th 2020, blog.idonethis.com/
distractions-at-work/

20 Gino Silva-Payne, "How to track and reduce your time spent on
email", Email Meter, July 15th 2020, www.emailmeter.com/blog/
track-time-spent-on-email

21 Jason Fried and David Heinemeier Hansson, *It Doesn't Have to be
Crazy at Work* (HarperCollins) 2018. The book is full of wisdom
but that didn't stop the writers from getting into controversy;
see Kim Lyons, "Basecamp CEO apologizes to staff in new post:
'We have a lot to learn'", Verge, May 4th 2021, www.theverge.
com/2021/5/4/22419799/basecamp-ceo-apologizes-staff-new-post

22 Gloria Mark et al., "Email duration, batching and self-interruption:
patterns of email use on productivity and stress", *MIT Media Lab*,
May 7th 2016, affect.media.mit.edu/pdfs/16.Mark-CHI_Email.pdf

23   "Workgeist report '21: research into culture, mindset and productivity for the modern work era", language.work, language.work/study/

24   Criado Perez, *Invisible Women*, op. cit.

25   James Citrin and Darleen DeRosa, *Leading at a Distance: Practical Lessons for Virtual Success* (Wiley) 2021

4 Jargon

1   The Orwell Foundation, "Politics and the English language", www.orwellfoundation.com/the-orwell-foundation/orwell/essays-and-other-works/politics-and-the-english-language/

2   Charlie Hoban et al., "It's time to drive impact", Oliver Wyman *Health Innovation Journal*, September 2019, www.oliverwyman.com/our-expertise/insights/2019/sep/health-innovation-journal/building-for-impact/its-time-to-drive-impact.html

3   John Authers, "If your CEO talks like Kant, think twice before investing", *Bloomberg Opinion*, September 17th 2021

4   Jenna Goudreau, "C is for Silly: the new C-suite titles", *Forbes*, January 10th 2012, www.forbes.com/sites/jennagoudreau/2012/01/10/c-is-for-silly-the-new-c-suite-titles/?sh=620687aa2a01

5   www.merriam-webster.com/dictionary/ideation

6   Shanna Davis, "Jargon genesis: 'think outside the box'", University of St Thomas, June 3rd 2010, news.stthomas.edu/jargon-genesis-think-outside-the-box/

7   Sports Lingo, www.sportslingo.com/sports-glossary/w/wheelhouse

5 Who would be a manager?

1   Laurence Peter and Raymond Hull, *The Peter Principle: Why Things Always Go Wrong* (William Morrow) 1969

2   Alan Benson, Danielle Li and Kelly Shue, "Promotions and the Peter principle", VoxEU, April 24th 2019

3   John Antonakis, Samuel Bendahan, Philippe Jacquart and Rafael

Lalive, "On making causal claims: a review and recommendations",
Leadership Quarterly, 21(6) 2010

4   Lananh Nguyen and Harry Wilson, "HSBC manager's heart attack
prompts viral post about overwork", *Bloomberg*, April 21st 2021

5   Charles Handy, *21 Letters on Life and Its Challenges* (Hutchinson)
2019

6   Ashleigh Webber, "Survey exposes burnout epidemic among
managers", *Personnel Today*, March 24th 2021

7   Martin Lindstrom, *The Ministry of Common Sense: How to
Eliminate Bureaucratic Red Tape, Bad Excuses, and Corporate BS*
(Houghton Mifflin Harcourt) 2021

6 The cult of the chief executive

1   John Preston, *Fall: The Mystery of Robert Maxwell* (Viking) 2021

2   "The palace of Versailles: Sun King Louis XIV's ultimate power
play", *History Extra,* www.historyextra.com/period/stuart/
palace-versailles-facts-history-court-sun-king-louis-xiv-france/

3   Jeff Cox, "CEOs see pay grow 1,000% in the last 40 years, now
make 278 times the average worker", CNBC, August 16th 2019,
www.cnbc.com/2019/08/16/ceos-see-pay-grow-1000percent-and-
now-make-278-times-the-average-worker.html

4   Nathan Brooks, quoted in "Corporate psychopaths common
and can wreak havoc in business, researcher says", Australian
Psychological Society, September 13th 2016, www.psychology.org.
au/news/media_releases/13September2016/Brooks/

5   Daniel Kahneman, *Thinking, Fast and Slow* (Penguin) 2012

6   Jeffrey Seglin, "The right thing: when executives say they don't have
a clue", *New York Times*, November 16th 2003

7   Schumpeter, "Will shareholders halt the inexorable rise of CEO
pay?", *The Economist*, May 15th 2021

8   Deborah Hargreaves, *Are Chief Executives Overpaid?* (Polity Books)
2018

9   "The risk of rewards: tailoring executive pay for long-term success",

FCLT Global Report, March 8th 2021, www.fcltglobal.org/
resource/executive-pay/

10   Robert Frank, "25 highest-paid hedge fund managers made $32
billion in 2020, a record", CNBC, February 22nd 2021, www.cnbc.
com/2021/02/22/-25-highest-paid-hedge-fund-managers-earned-
record-setting-32-billion-in-2020.html

11   Patrick Temple-West, "US investors revolt against pay in record
numbers", *Financial Times*, May 10th 2021

7 Modern managers

1   Jim Clifton and Jim Harter, *It's the Manager: Moving from Boss to
Coach* (Gallup Press) 2019

2   Ibid.

3   Stefanie Lange et al., "Workplace bullying among employees in
Germany: prevalence estimates and the role of the perpetrator",
International Archives of Occupational and Environmental Health
92(8) February 2019

4   Clive Lewis, *Toxic: A Guide to Rebuilding Respect and Tolerance in a
Hostile Workplace* (Bloomsbury Business) 2021

5   Tom Peters and Robert Waterman, *In Search of Excellence: Lessons
from America's Best-Run Companies* (Harper & Row) 1982

6   Amy Edmondson, *The Fearless Organization: Creating Psychological
Safety in the Workplace for Learning, Innovation, and Growth*
(Wiley) 2018

7   Jack Welch, "Jack Welch: 'Rank-and-Yank'? That's not how it's
done", *WSJ Opinion*, November 14th 2013

8   Jan Woike and Sebastian Hafenbrädl, "Rivals without a cause?
Relative performance feedback creates destructive competition
despite aligned incentives", *Journal of Behavioral Decision Making*
33(4), February 12th 2020

9   Ting Zhang et al., "Reducing bounded ethicality: how to help
individuals notice and avoid unethical behaviour", *Organizational
Dynamics* 44(4) October – December 2015

10   Clifton and Harter, *It's the Manager*, op. cit.

11   Lori Nishiura Mackenzie, JoAnne Wehner and Sofia Kennedy,
     "How do you evaluate performance during a pandemic?",
     Harvard Business Review, December 7th 2020, hbr.org/2020/12/
     how-do-you-evaluate-performance-during-a-pandemic

12   Angelo DeNisi and Avraham Kluger, "Feedback effectiveness: can
     360-degree appraisals be improved?", *Academy of Management
     Executive* 14(1) February 2000

13   Clifton and Harter, *It's the Manager*, op. cit.

14   "Toyota production system: maximising production efficiency
     through the elimination of waste", www.toyota-europe.com/
     world-of-toyota/this-is-toyota/toyota-production-system

15   Alex Edmans, "How great companies deliver both purpose and
     profit", London Business School, October 31st 2019, www.london.
     edu/think/how-great-companies-deliver-both-purpose-and-profit

16   David Bodanis, *The Art of Fairness: The Power of Decency in a World
     Turned Mean* (Bridge Street Press) 2021

17   "William Baumol, a great economist, died on May 4th", *The
     Economist*, May 13th 2017

18   Eric Schmidt, Jonathan Rosenberg and Alan Eagle, *Trillion Dollar
     Coach: The Leadership Handbook of Silicon Valley's Bill Campbell*
     (Harper Business) 2019

19   Murad Ahmed, "Euro 2020: Gareth Southgate's meticulous
     approach makes England contenders again", *Financial Times*, July
     10th 2021

20   Gareth Southgate, "Dear England", *Players' Tribune*,
     June 8th 2021, www.theplayerstribune.com/posts/
     dear-england-gareth-southgate-euros-soccer

21   Adam Smith, *An Inquiry into the Nature and Causes of the Wealth of
     Nations* (W. Strahan and T. Cadell) 1776

22   Paul Polman and Andrew Winston, *Net Positive: How Courageous
     Companies Thrive by Giving More than They Take* (Harvard Business
     Review Press) 2021

23   Milton Friedman, "A Friedman doctrine – the social responsibility

of business is to increase its profits", *New York Times*, September
13th 1970

24 "Academics make an empirical case against stakeholderism", *The Economist*, March 14th 2020

25 Enron, "Statement of human rights principles", www.csus.edu/indiv/m/merlinos/enron.html

26 "Climate change has made ESG a force in investing", *The Economist*, December 7th 2019

27 Tensie Whelan et al., "ESG and financial performance: uncovering the relationship by aggregating evidence from 1,000 plus studies published between 2015 – 2020", NYU Stern Center for Sustainable Business, February 2021, www.stern.nyu.edu/experience-stern/about/departments-centers-initiatives/centers-of-research/center-sustainable-business/research/research-initiatives/esg-and-financial-performance

8 Helping hands

1 "Market size of the global consulting industry in 2020?", consultancy.uk, May 26th 2020, www.consultancy.uk/news/24659/market-size-of-the-global-consulting-industry-in-2020

2 Tom Bolger and Casey Foss, "How to tell if hiring a consultant will be worth the investment", *Harvard Business Review*, May 24th 2021, hbr.org/sponsored/2021/05/how-to-tell-if-hiring-a-consultant-will-be-worth-the-investment

3 Stanford GSB staff, "Economics Lessons From Indian Textile Firms", December 24th 2010, www.gsb.stanford.edu/insights/research-economics-lessons-indian-textile-firms

4 Linda Childers Hon, "Demonstrating effectiveness in public relations: goals, objectives, and evaluation", *Journal of Public Relations Research* 10(2) 1998

5 Dennis Tourish, *Management Studies in Crisis: Fraud, Deception and Meaningless Research* (Cambridge University Press) 2019

6 Ibid.

7 Raymond Hubbard, *Corrupt Research: The Case for*

Reconceptualizing Empirical Management and Social Science (Sage) 2015

8   "Spurious correlations", tylervigen.com, www.tylervigen.com/ spurious-correlations

9   Tourish, *Management Studies in Crisis*, op. cit.

10   "American business schools are reinventing the MBA", *The Economist*, November 2nd 2019

11   Ibid.

12   Jeff Schmitt, "Asian business schools: pay, satisfaction & diversity", *Poets & Quants*, May 15th 2021, poetsandquants.com/2021/05/15/ asian-business-schools-pay-satisfaction-and-diversity/

13   Eva Ranehill et al., "Assessing the robustness of power posing: no effect on hormones and risk tolerance in a large sample of men and women", *Psychological Science* 26(5) 2015

9 The future of work. Part 1

1   John Maynard Keynes, "Economic possibilities for our grandchildren (1930)" in *Essays in Persuasion* (W. W. Norton & Co.) 1963, http://www.econ.yale.edu/smith/econ116a/keynes1.pdf

2   Jonathan Ponciano, "The Forbes 400 self-made score: from silver spooners to bootstrappers", Forbes, September 8th 2020

3   WHO/ILO, "Long working hours increasing deaths from heart disease and stroke: WHO, ILO", May 17th 2021, www.who.int/ news/item/17-05-2021-long-working-hours-increasing-deaths-from-heart-disease-and-stroke-who-ilo

4   Brendan Burchell et al., "Cut hours, not people: no work, furlough, short hours and mental health during the COVID-19 pandemic in the UK", *Understanding Society*, July 15th 2020, www. understandingsociety.ac.uk/research/publications/526206

5   Sarah Kessler, *Gigged: The Gig Economy, the End of the Job and the Future of Work* (Random House Business) 2018

6   "William Lee invents the stocking frame knitting machine, the first stage in the mechanization of textiles", History of Information, www.historyofinformation.com/detail.php?entryid=3634

7   Sarah Laskow, "A machine that made stockings helped kick off the Industrial Revolution", Atlas Obscura, September 19th 2017, www.atlasobscura.com/articles/machine-silk-stockings-industrial-revolution-queen-elizabeth

8   Carl Benedikt Frey and Michael Osborne, "The future of employment: how susceptible are jobs to computerisation?", Oxford Martin School, September 17th 2013, www.oxfordmartin.ox.ac.uk/downloads/academic/future-of-employment.pdf

9   Michael Osborne and Carl Benedikt Frey, "Automation and the future of work – understanding the numbers", Oxford Martin School, April 13th 2018, www.oxfordmartin.ox.ac.uk/blog/automation-and-the-future-of-work-understanding-the-numbers/

10   Daniel Susskind, *A World Without Work: Technology, Automation and How We Should Respond* (Metropolitan Books) 2020

11   Robert Bootle, *The AI Economy: Work, Wealth and Welfare in the Age of the Robot* (Nicholas Brealey) 2019

12   Lauren Seay and Mahum Tofiq, "US banks shutter record number of branches in 2020", S&P Global Market Intelligence, January 15th 2021, www.spglobal.com/marketintelligence/en/news-insights/latest-news-headlines/us-banks-shutter-record-number-of-branches-in-2020-62083337

13   Graph of "Employment rate: aged 15–64: all persons for the United States", Federal Reserve Bank of St Louis, October 2021, fred.stlouisfed.org/series/LREM64TTUSM156S

14   "How will automation affect jobs, skills, and wages?", McKinsey Global Institute, March 23rd 2018, www.mckinsey.com/featured-insights/future-of-work/how-will-automation-affect-jobs-skills-and-wages

15   www.weforum.org/press/2020/10/recession-and-automation-changes-our-future-of-work-but-there-are-jobs-coming-report-says-52c5162fce/

16   "*Robo sapiens*: future of work primer", privately circulated research note, May 12th 2021

17 Max Roser, "Employment in agriculture", OurWorldInData.org, 2013, ourworldindata.org/employment-in-agriculture

18 "Employment by industry, 1910 and 2015", *TED: The Economics Daily*, March 3rd 2016, www.bls.gov/opub/ted/2016/employment-by-industry-1910-and-2015.htm

19 Callum Williams, "The future of work", *The Economist*, April 10th 2021

20 OECD. Source: stats.oecd.org/Index.aspx?DataSetCode=POPPROJ#

21 Federal Reserve Bank of New York, *SCE Labor Market Survey*, www.newyorkfed.org/microeconomics/sce/labor#/expectations-job-search16

22 Williams, "The future of work", op. cit.

10 The future of work. Part 2

1   "What harm do minimum wages do?", *The Economist*, August 15th 2020

2   Williams, "The future of work", op. cit.

3   "What harm do minimum wages do?", op. cit.

4   Helena Vieira, "National minimum wages improve productivity", LSE, January 18th 2017, blogs.lse.ac.uk/businessreview/2017/01/18/national-minimum-wages-improve-productivity/

5   "Tax wedge", OECD Date, data.oecd.org/tax/tax-wedge.htm

6   Lorenzo Bernal-Verdugo, Davide Furceri and Dominique Guillaume, "Labor market flexibility and unemployment: new empirical evidence of static and dynamic effects", *IMF Working Paper*, March 2012

7   Kessler, *Gigged*, op. cit.

8   Ronald Coase, "The nature of the firm", *Economica* 4(16) 1937

9   "Coase's theory of the firm", *The Economist*, July 29th 2017

10 "Almost two-fifths of working adults given less than a week's notice of working hours", Living Wage Foundation, www.livingwage.org.uk/news/almost-two-fifths-working-adults-given-less-week%E2%80%99s-notice-working-hours

11 Thor Berger et al., "Uber happy? Work and well-being in the 'gig economy'", *Economic Policy* 34(99) July 2019

12 David Graeber, *Bullshit Jobs: A Theory* (Allen Lane) 2018

13 Magdalena Soffia, Alex Wood and Brendan Burchell, "Alienation is not 'bullshit': an empirical critique of Graeber's theory of BS jobs", *Work, Employment and Society*, June 2021

14 "European offices: working from home for longer (still)", privately circulated research note, April 13th 2021

15 CIPD, "More employers reporting increased productivity benefits from homeworking compared to last summer, new CIPD research finds", April 1st 2021, www.cipd.co.uk/about/media/press/010421homeworking-increased-productivity#gref

16 Michael Gibbs, Friederike Mengel and Christoph Siemroth, "Work from home & productivity: evidence from personnel & analytics data on IT professionals", *BFI Working Paper*, July 13th 2021, bfi.uchicago.edu/wp-content/uploads/2021/05/BFI_WP_2021-56.pdf

17 Leanna Byrne, "Working from home job adverts rise", BBC News, August 11th 2021, www.bbc.co.uk/news/business-58160245

18 "Remote-first work is taking over the rich world", *The Economist*, October 30th 2021

19 Daniel Kahneman and Alan Krueger, "Developments in the measurement of subjective well-being", *Journal of Economic Perspectives* 20(1) 2006

20 Felix Richter, "Cars still dominate the American commute", Statista, May 29th 2019, www.statista.com/chart/18208/means-of-transportation-used-by-us-commuters/#:~:text=According%20to%20Statista's%20Global%20Consumer,most%20popular%20way%20of%20commuting

21 "Google may cut pay of staff who work from home", BBC News, August 11th 2021, www.bbc.co.uk/news/business-58171716

22 "Women in the workplace 2021", McKinsey & Co., September 27th 2021, www.mckinsey.com/featured-insights/diversity-and-inclusion/women-in-the-workplace

23 Jillian Smith, "Envoy survey finds hybrid work improves mental

health for UK workers", Envoy blog, May 26th 2021, envoy.com/
blog/envoy-survey-finds-hybrid-work-improves-mental-health-for-
uk-workers

24 Charlotte Gascoigne, "Flexible working: lessons from the
pandemic", CIPD, April 2021, www.cipd.co.uk/Images/flexible-
working-lessons-from-pandemic-report_tcm18-92644.pdf

ACKNOWLEDGEMENTS

This book is based on the Bartleby column at *The Economist*, where I had the privilege to work for 15 years. Thanks are due to Tamzin Booth, Jan Piotrowski, Matthew Valencia and Patrick Foulis who edited the column at various stages and a special mention is due for Liz Mann, Michael Coulman and the team of fact checkers who weeded out innumerable errors. I am grateful that Zanny Minton Beddoes chose me to write the column and Edward Carr hired me for *The Economist* in the first place.

At Profile, thanks are due to Ed Lake and Andrew Franklin, who started me on the bumpy road of book writing back in 1985 and to Clare Grist Taylor for her astute editing suggestions. Last of all, I am immensely grateful to Sandie, Helena and Catherine for their loving support.